It's About Love After All

Essays on Child Welfare

Hon. Sherri Sobel, Ret.

Dedication

For the children, especially mine—Abby & Ian, who raised me. And the icing on the cake—Bennet.

This is a truth-based non-fiction-ish book. Some families' stories are merged and all the names in this book have changed.

*You've got to have something to eat, and a little love in your life
before you can hold still for any damn body's
sermon on how to behave.*

—Billie Holiday

Table of Contents

Prologue

How the Child Welfare System Came to Be
and Where We Are Today

One of the inalienable rights described by our Constitution is the right to parent your children without government interference. For most of our country's history, there was no welfare, and absolutely no child welfare.

Around the turn of the twentieth century, the first protective laws were passed. The first court case concerned children of a religious sect who had spent hours on the street begging, after which they took cash home to their parents. Children were working long hours, but eventually laws were passed to protect children from being exploited ten, twelve, fifteen hours a day.

Finally, grappling with the issue of protection of children to be free from abuse in the home, there was Stanley v. Illinois, 405 U.S. 645 (1972), which held that the right to parent was so important that it required strict scrutiny, the highest level of right, before the government could intervene. It was a landmark United States Supreme Court case in which the Court held that the fathers of children born out of wedlock had a fundamental right to their children.

So started the child welfare system.

As time went on, departments of social services sprung up, as an alternative to police action, in order to provide more enlightened responses to possible abuse. The removal of children was almost unheard of, the provision of family assistance was the template.

In modern times, we cannot imagine a world where abused children must remain in abusive homes. We remove them, provide parents a certain amount of time to readjust their lives, and then either return the children or place them in a permanent home which is not their family of origin. But the overarching theme of child welfare has always been to try to reunite every child either with natural parents or within the family structure, meaning appropriate relatives.

As it stands, more grandparents than ever are raising grandchildren in this country, with numbers varying from four million to fifteen million. This does not include the aunts, uncles, cousins, and older siblings who come forward and take care of these kids.

We miss some instances of real child abuse or neglect due mostly to uncaring adults, unaware schools, and overworked social workers, or family secrets. Most of us in the system always try our best with what we know. We wish we didn't have to separate families, but we do so to protect the children. We work hard to reunite them, if in the best interest of the child.

In America, we try to keep family first, parents and children as a unit, free from government interference.

All we can do is try to help every single child who enters our foster care system.

1

What Do Young Children
Understand in a Courtroom?

I watch children come into court. They come in in a variety of ways. Either with their parents, relatives, or county drivers; on probation; from downstairs in our shelter care; or from their foster homes. They come into court, and they are given teddy bears, and coloring pages with crayons. Their parents come in, and mostly, their interactions are subdued. I allowed hugs and kisses before we got started, and also sitting on laps. We cater the hearings to the children; if I had negative things to say, I asked that the children be removed from the court. I checked with them, as to the placement, school, interests, all depending on age. I was so careful to not upset the fragility of their current lives, and kept my voice as even as I could when they were in the room. The older the children were, the less careful I was, sometimes prompting an outburst on the parent's behalf from the child.

So what? What did it matter, mostly, when they were not going home? There were children for whom this was not an issue, but they were very few. What did they hear? What did they misinterpret?

When I talked to the parents about drug treatment, did they hear the word "treat"? Or were they aware, even at a young age, of drugs, and what they could do? Some children as young as four or five described the white powder Mom smells. Or the smell of marijuana in their home. "Oh, that's just weed," I was told.

Did these young children understand why they couldn't go home? They did not cry or yell at me. Their lawyers all prefaced their recommendation with the fact they wanted to go home, then let me know they did not think the parents were ready.

What did they think we were doing? Did they understand, the little ones, why they were in this situation? Did they understand my words? Sometimes, even the parents did not hear me right. They asked, after I'd made my ruling that the children were not going home, when they could pick them up. I have found I had not made myself clear whenever I was trying to be kind.

In front of the children, I praised the parents for whatever I could find to praise, so it was somewhat understandable they thought I was sending their children home. I saved the anger for when the children were not in the room. Did that mean they were confused, since I praised the parents but wouldn't let them go home?

I wrestled always with the care of words I used. I was very hands on, avoiding too much aloof legal language in my decisions. I based my decisions on case law, on statute, on Federal findings I made, but after looking into the faces before me, and talking to them in a language that I hoped got through, I bargained, I promised, I refused to promise, I used carrot, and I used stick. I wanted the parents to leave with no hesitation as to what it would take to get their children back home.

But what could the children do to help that? What did they hear me say in a court about children, that gave them any clue as to what they could do to impact the outcome of their lives? It was the layer of Juvie that did not get solved.

What do the children hear?

2

Why We Do Anything

When I was seventeen, I started college. I lived at home and commuted to Temple University in Philly. I was close friends with Jackie, a girl from high school who was in my same teaching major.

One day, Jackie said that Pablo Casals was performing in the small music amphitheater. It was a teaching exercise, and it would be free for us to attend. We were going for sure, even though I thought, "Pablo who?" My parents loved music and we had music playing constantly in the house: blues, spirituals, pop, rock, and folk. Miriam Makeba, Ella Fitzgerald, Frank Sinatra, Satchmo, Louis Prima, and Keely Smith. But no classical music. Oh well, what the heck. I was game.

Jackie and I sat in the bleachers. In the center, on a small floor stage, was a wizened old man with a cello. Next to him was a young female student, also with a cello. It turns out I was watching the most famous cello player in the world give a lesson to a new music student. She played a piece. It was beautiful. When she finished, there was a respectable applause. Then Mr. Casals played the same piece. It was ethereal, haunting, magnificent. We were silent. By performance end, the young student was openly sobbing. Mr. Casals leaned over, took her hand, and placed it on his heart. With a strong accent, he said, "I want to feel your passion." Something in me heard that to my bones.

Oh yes! Do it with passion, or do not do it at all. I could not tell if doing something you had to do, or something you wanted to do, should be separated from that axiom. I just know that those wise words from Mr. Casals informed the rest of my life choices. One of my other favorite mottoes, said by a Philadelphia radio personality, was, "Often wrong, never in doubt." So my life motto became, "Often wrong, never in doubt, full speed ahead!"

I married young and had children young. I often think back on the many mistakes I made. My children essentially raised me, and have turned out to be simply wonderful humans. But I thought that I would like to expend that passion in the service of other children, maybe to do it better than I did with my own guinea pigs. Thus, I entered law school, took the bar, and began a career in juvenile court, at a not so-young-age of thirty-six.

I do not believe one can successfully navigate the emotional toll of Juvie without passion. I must feel I am the best "Jewish Mother" there is. Chicken soup for all, with a healthy dose of nagging and guilt to wash it down. I talk to my parents in court as if I were the parent they did not have. I talk to the kids at length to discover their passions, and I help them articulate a plan to take them to their goals. I remind them that the number one goal is to never have their children in my court. Thank you. To substitute personal goals for emptiness, and empower them to strive for and achieve those goals. In other words, I want to see their passion. It is the best part of my job. It is the silver lining of a very dark cloud.

I hope that Mr. Casals's student persevered with her music, and didn't give up. I hope she found that passion, and let it lift her up. I found mine.

3

The Car Ride That Changed My Life

I have worked with young people in two different fields: education and Juvie. Because of our backgrounds, I could not relate to them. I cannot imagine the lives that they were born into through no fault of their own. I have never lost sight of this fact.

I came to Juvie after a career spent outside the field, working as an English teacher at an all-boys school in inner city Philadelphia. I had done some student teaching in two areas that were somewhat related to the work I do now. One short semester in a suburban setting, one semester in an urban setting, just up the street from my college, Temple University. I loved the kids in the suburban junior high, but I really resonated with the urban, mostly minority kids in the inner city. Back then, in 1965, you had to take a teacher's exam after you received your diploma, and those tests would be ranked. Luckily, I ranked very highly. According to the ranking, you were interviewed and matched to a school. The higher the ranking, the more choices you had for assignment. I chose Benjamin Franklin High School, on Broad Street in Philly. There were some raised eyebrows, especially since I had graduated at age twenty and weighed a fast ninety pounds soaking wet on my four-foot-eleven frame. Ben Franklin was an all-boys school, and some of the students were close to my age. But I felt right being there when I did student teaching. I wanted to go back.

I loved teaching. I loved my kids. I loved their joy and ability to have fun in the midst of some chaos all around them. They were poor. They were in gangs. We were in the midst of a civil rights movement that brought celebrities and civil rights movement advocates like H. Rap Brown, Sammy Davis Jr., and Nancy Wilson to the school to inspire the students.

One night, I was driving some of my kids to the theater. We had gotten tickets donated for a play in town, and I was one of the chaperones. Halfway to the theater, we were stopped by a police car. I asked the policeman why we had been stopped, expecting a broken taillight or some such. However, his questions made it apparent that he was concerned about a white woman driving a car full of boys who were not white. I assured the officer that I was fine, and we went on our way. I was marked, indelibly, with the wrongness of that encounter, the kids' knowledge of it, and how really dumb I was about race in America.

Unlike the kids in Juvie, I lived in my row home from birth to adulthood. There with me were my father, my mother, and my sister, Judy. My father's family emigrated to the United States from Russia in 1904. I don't know the details about my mother's family, but I believe they emigrated from Romania. Both sides of the family came to escape the pogroms against Jews and start a new life in America. First, the neighborhood. It was safe, clean, heavenly. At the end of my street was Freda and Al's, which was a good old-fashioned candy store with an ice cream fountain, and in the back room they served hamburgers and fries. Around that corner, there was a pharmacist, kosher meat market, and grocery store. There was no such thing as a supermarket until I was about ten, when the first A&P opened in our neighborhood. All in all, my family's needs were met within walking distance. There was no graffiti, no homeless people sleeping on the streets or open-air drug usage where I grew up.

I took growing up in a good neighborhood for granted as I knew no other reality at the time. I was never scared walking down any streets in my town, partly because it was safe and also because I always had people around me. Growing up, I had a big circle of girlfriends and lovely boys we traded off dating. Almost all of us were Jewish, nearly all destined for college, and all had about the same financial situation.

My friends walked around everywhere together, whether it was to school or to home from school in enough time to watch *Bandstand* with Dick Clark, at that time a local show, and we'd all dance until dinner. Then there was homework, an hour with girlfriends on the phone, and bed. On the weekends, we went shopping, mostly window shopping, or took a long walk to the nearest park. Then back to my house, where the kids gathered. We had a finished basement with knotty pine walls and the latest 45s.

At no time did I ever feel unsafe, day or night.

My friends weren't the only ones who kept me company. There was also my family. On my mother's side, there were seven uncles and aunts, seventeen first cousins, all close and hilarious. All my friends knew at least some of my cousins. With in-laws and close friends, holidays at my Aunt Roz's could run to fifty or more. Seders, Thanksgiving. It was the same turnout when we'd all spend a week at my grandfather's hotel in Atlantic City, and a week at my Aunt Ann's socialist camp called "Nature Friends." My aunt and her husband were socialists, and the camp was a wonderful, informal family camp. If anyone talked politics, the kids didn't hear it. I do know the camp was closed by some government entity.

My dad's family was one generation removed from the Russian pogroms (think *Fiddler on the Roof*). There were five kids, and they were much quieter than Mom's side. Every Friday, we would all go to my Bubbe's house for Sabbath dinner.

Now, were we a perfect family? No. Like every family, we had our troubles. There were drugs, divorces, job problems, some brushes with the law. In other words, we had some similar problems just like the families who would appear before me in court some forty years later. But in our family, when someone was messing up, we all knew about it. There was no such thing as isolation in our big family. We not only knew what was going on, but some of us always stepped up to try to do something about it. There was always some family member who tried to help until the problem was solved. Whatever life problems arose in our family, it always worked out. Why? Because our family never gave up on any one of us. The whole family. Aunt would call aunt, cousin called cousin, and whatever it was, the problem was supported until it was fixed.

It's the same now as it was then but now we are on our fourth generation, spread out over the whole country. The last time my big family were mostly all together was at my Aunt Reba's hundredth birthday. When we gathered it was as if we had seen each other yesterday. All the uncles and aunts are gone now, and even three of the cousins. So much time had passed when we all got together again. The spindly trees planted on our curbs are now grown trees canopying the street I grew up on.

Looking back on my own childhood, I realized how lucky I was. My outcome from a good childhood is that I have healthy and fabulous children and a grandchild. Growing up and older, I saw throughout my life that whenever friends and family encountered a life problem, what they needed was each other. And these problems, no matter what they were, would get resolved when there was family and friend support. Decades later, I would think about these things, and that car ride that changed my life. I subconsciously draw parallels to my own childhood when I worked with families. If it takes a village, I surely had mine. Seeing all that the Juvie families didn't have in comparison to what I had growing up helped me better understand why so many families struggle to this day.

4

Juvie Can Show Up When You Least Expect It

I was forty when I took and passed the bar. Through a series of very lucky breaks, I found myself at Juvie. I was in the right place, at the right time, with the right people.

So there I was, a complete newbie, fresh out of law school, my bar card crisp and bright, and I was wearing my best big girl outfit. I was pretty nervous, and had absolutely no idea what I was getting into. I started on the same day as an acquaintance from law school named Rhoda. We both looked like we stepped into Alice's Wonderland without either the rabbit or the cake.

One of the first things I did on my first day as a lawyer was walk to my court administrator Annette's cubicle. Annette ruled the world from a closet. She handed out the files that became our cases. We lawyers lined up, and out the files came. She'd hand files to us lawyers and tell us the gist of what we needed to hear: "You, here is the father, here is the mother, we have five kids, who once lived with grandma, another mother, another father." I picked up children, or the alleged perpetrator of abuse, or a parent or parents who neglected their children to buy and use alcohol. Or drugs. Domestic violence, physical abuse, filthy homes, filthy children, broken bones, beatings, anything and everything you could imagine when the cases were handed to us.

I was expected to read the charges on the petition and the accompanying screening summary, then see my client and prepare to represent him or her, or the children. I had not one iota of the relevant law or the Welfare and the Institution Code. Never heard of it, never was taught it in law school, I barely knew where to find it. Thankfully, I ran into Candy, another law school acquaintance who was good enough to point me in the right direction.

My strategy was to use common sense, use the Welfare and the Institution Code book, and try to get the kids home if I had a parent, or do what was best for the kids, if I represented them. Each representation required a different hat, and different strategies. Chess on steroids, moving real people around a real playing board. I thanked Candy for helping me as we headed for my first courtroom. I yelled for my client in the chaos of twenty lawyers all talking at once to their twenty clients in a small, dark hallway. I asked their side of the facts in the petition, which was almost always different than what was written down, then prepared my arguments to try to either get the kids home, or pave the way as soon as possible. Jailed clients were brought into special rooms to be interviewed. I'd ask them if they had any relatives? Were they there? Lawyers who represented parents when I represented the kids came to me to try to convince me to argue with them to return the children home and vice versa. I loved every minute of it. The whole scene just fit who I was, but several hours later, I ran into Rhoda, who looked frazzled and miserable at the end of her first day. She looked at me and said

"Not in this lifetime," she said as she handed me her files. I never saw her again. But my new career was off and running. I had an office, business cards, a briefcase, a secretary (shared), and my own telephone. Wow.

Several months later, with over a hundred clients, my own Code book, and a pretty good handle on things, I realized my stomach was not enjoying this line of work as much as my brain was. It got bad enough that my doctor referred me to Scripps Hospital for tests. I checked in, and had a GI series done. I was ushered into the office of a lovely gray-haired gentleman. He was a gastroenterologist who had read my x-rays. He told me that he saw no problems and that I was in good health. I asked him facetiously if I should call Deepak Chopra, a famous doctor of meditation in San Diego.

The good doctor replied, "What would a lovely housewife have to be stressed over?"

Somewhat offended, I asked him, "What makes you think I'm a housewife?"

He commented on my clothes, age, and demeanor. I proceeded to tell him what I did for a living. His eyes got bigger and bigger. He said he was surprised I didn't have an ulcer. He then did something I will never forget.

"Can you give me some pointers on what to look for when it comes to possible abuse?" He then explained that medical schools did not teach many classes on the subject of child abuse, and he thought they should. I left that appointment with us both having learned something; he learned something new, and I began some necessary stress reduction.

Juvie, it touches us all.

In another related story, I called my ex-husband, a radiologist, to ask him to read x-rays for a boy I represented, a three-year-old with a broken leg. His mother said she sat on him by accident. Since she was morbidly obese, I thought it was possible. He gave me his opinion, which was "maybe," and then said, "You know, we aren't taught any of this in medical school, or residency, and I think we should. I see broken bones all the time, and I think some patients should be alerted to possible child abuse, or domestic violence."

Juvie, it touches us all.

And another time, I took my cat to the vet for her to get her shots. In idle conversation, the vet and I got to talking about my job, which we had not done before. When I told him that I represent children and families in juvenile court, he said, "You know, they should be teaching us how to recognize abuse in animals brought to us." Since animal abuse can be a precursor to child abuse or domestic violence, I agreed with him.

Juvie, it touches us all.

5

From Hotline Call to First Hearing

Here is a roadmap of how our families end up in the first hearing. First comes a hotline referral. Or a call from a teacher, a therapist, or some other mandated reporter. This call triggers an in-person response. The Department sends out a social worker or two to either the school or home to evaluate the situation.

At this point, there are a number of available options. The social worker can determine that the report was unfounded, and close the file. The social worker can also determine that the report had some merit and make a referral to community services that would work for the family. The social worker can determine that the report is founded, but the family is motivated to make the necessary changes to support safety for the children. The Department can then work with the family by providing oversight and services without filing a petition. If the family complies with the voluntary contract, there is no case. If, however, they do not, then a petition is filed.

Then there are the families where there is a need for judicial intervention. There are two ways this petition is filed. One way is that the petition is non-detained, which means the children are not removed from the family home. The children are not detained away from the family. The second way is that there is a detained petition. If there is clear and articulable current danger to the children, and there are no services that could ameliorate that danger, the children are removed and detained with a relative or in a foster home. The Department of Children and Family Services has forty-eight hours to decide.

Twenty-four hours after the detained petition is filed, in court, at the first hearing I hear arguments regarding that removal. I must make the findings that the removal is legally permissible. So the parents, and possibly the children's counsel, argue that there is no reason for removal, based on their reading of the original facts, or that there are indeed services that could allow the children to safely return home while the case is pending. This is a crucial part of my job. The children, for the most part, are desperate to be home. Besides the obvious reasons, their friends are there, their school is there, their teddy bear is there. I carefully listen to the arguments, but usually, I know what I will do by reading the paperwork prepared by the social worker. I have read those reports long before I see the family. Sometimes, however, I am persuaded by seeing the family before me, where I get a different picture than that painted by the Department. I sometimes go with my gut. Sometimes I am right. Also, sometimes I am wrong! Either side can appeal my ruling; however, that is rare at this early stage.

In court, I evaluate the demeanor of the parents. I evaluate the demeanor of the kids. Can I send the older kids home, as school is so important, or do I send the youngest home, as bonding and attachment are so important? Do I split the children up?

Some of these issues are somewhat decided for me—a little easier—when a previously non-custodial parent shows up at court and is ready, willing, and able to provide a safe and stable home for his or her child. However those types of scenarios work out, I have now split up that family on the first day, probably for the long haul. Siblings raised together, no matter how awful the circumstances are, or probably because they have gone through the same devastation, cling to each other.

But there is an even worse experience in store for me. There are times when, for whatever reason—fear, laziness, inexperience—the social worker leaves the children at home, and without telling the parent, asks me to remove the children in court. Or, horribly, the decision is made to keep the kids at home, and the Department stands by that decision. The family shows up, somewhat chastened, anxious to convince me that they are willing to do whatever they need to do. The abuser has moved out, and agrees to voluntarily stay away. The victim asks for a restraining order. A drug test has been taken, and is clean. The parent is in a program already.

So I ask myself, how many times has the parent been asked to get the abuser out? How many times has he or she moved back in? How many drug programs started and abandoned? Restraining orders ignored? Are the kids in school? Do they get there every day? Who makes breakfast? Is anyone working? Are the older kids raising the younger? Is the appropriate physical discipline the result of background or differences in country-of-origin practices? Is it a hand or a fist? Electric cord, paddle, or shoe? Is there an articulate nexus between the punishment and the child's behavior? Or just the anger of an out-of-control parent? I ask myself these questions and then I rule, with the children in the room.

Oftentimes, the courtroom erupts. The children begin to scream. They clutch their parents, and each other. They try to run out of the courtroom, and are restrained by the social workers called up to transport them away from the court by another exit, to other homes. If possible, I try to keep them together. But there are not many foster homes that will take five, six children of very disparate ages. I make visitation orders to ensure that they see each other with their parents several times a week. It does not help. One young man, fifteen, says he has been the primary caretaker for his two-year-old brother, and they will die without each other. Many older children have been the guardians of their mothers through a continuing line of abusive men. They plead with me that the next one could kill her without them being there to intervene. They're so used to being the adult in the family.

I try to remind all those children that they are entitled to be children, and I make orders to transport them back to their schools when I can, to try to at least let them see their friends.

When these types of hearings are over, I am exhausted, and drained. Yet I still have enough left over to cry. I do cry sometimes. But with hope.

6

The Three Types of Lawyers That Exist in Juvie

There is an old legal maxim: "When you have the facts, pound the facts. When you have the law, pound the law. When you have neither, pound the table."

One of the hardest things to do as a judge was not so much to judge the poor possible perpetrators before me; it was to stop judging the lawyers. Depending on what we did before the bench, we on the bench all pretty much thought we could do a better job in comparison. Part of my job was to keep this comparison to myself and not let it jeopardize my decision.

But sometimes it was hard.

I once had a lawyer, Ann, who was so obnoxious that she just scraped me raw. Everything was a constitutional issue, requiring an argument at high pitch and long wind. Finally, after one session where I labored, in vain, to shorten her diatribe, I simply told her I was going off the record, and let her know that she was talking to a wall. Next stop, I could get off the bench and go into my chambers, but that I felt was disrespectful to her client, and I did not want to do it.

Ann shut up, then said that she hoped my anger at her did not affect my treatment of her client. I told her that, in fact, I liked her client. I left it at that.

In my decades of experience, I have seen that lawyers come in three types. Kind of like the three bears with their porridge. Papa Bear was always too hot, Mama Bear was always too cold, and Baby Bear was just right.

Allow me to elaborate with this analogy.

With the Papa Bear lawyers, they spent a lot of time pounding the table. It was always someone else's fault: the Department, other family members, the service providers, anyone other than his client. Since the behavior of the parent was usually the impetus for the petition in the first place, and defensiveness the first reaction, this strategy was guaranteed to make the client dig in his or her heels, and in response, all providers did the same. Bad outcomes ensued. If the lawyer continued to argue that the parent did nothing wrong, the parent had no impetus to improve.

Mama Bear lawyers were the opposite. They didn't fight at all. No trials ever got set. No matter how much wiggle room there could be in a plea, or subsequent recommendations, those lawyers were quick to take anyone's suggestion but her or his clients'. "My client is sorry," was typically the go-to phrase. The client wasn't the only sorry one. Feeling like one was never heard was the too real experiences of our families. Having a do-nothing lawyer only exasperated the problem. The parent was discouraged, and without strong support in the community, and then the courtroom, he or she usually ended up either disappearing or relapsing. Having no advocacy also gave no impetus to improve.

Then there were the Baby Bear lawyers who were just right. These lawyers did triage when the case came in. They examined the petition and determined what issues to argue and not argue. A strong and capable conversation with the client then came next. They would tell their clients, "You will own this, and get started into services now," and, "This is arguable, we will argue or set a trial to either get rid of or modify that count." They were in charge of their clients, and their client trusted that the lawyer would act in their best interests. For my part, I recognized a Baby Bear lawyer when I heard a reasoned and calmly delivered presentation. Those parents were often lucky and mostly successful. I hope I was a Baby Bear lawyer.

7

The Differences Between Lawyering and Judging

Law school was like heaven to me. I was a natural debater from childhood, so being encouraged to argue was really manna. I got to argue with teachers for credit. I wrote arguments and was graded on them. Manna. Generally, people who go to law school are like me. What law school teaches us is that every issue has two sides, and a good lawyer can argue either side. We learn to dissect precedent, read dissents, and parse, parse, parse. We glory in esoteric dissertations and drive our friends crazy. Then we take the bar, and pass, and now get paid to argue.

Manna.

I was lucky enough to meet someone who steered me to Juvie right away. I was living in San Diego at the time. We practiced law in the British style, which means we were assigned cases neutrally, representing any party as the cases came in. Typically, law practice is one side only. I represented a parent on one case, a child on another, and I had many cases both for children and for parents. When I represented one parent, I could bad mouth the other side with impunity; I took an oath to zealously represent my client. It was a time of real learning about people with real problems. The people I represented, and fought against, had a variety of attitudes, from fear to belligerence, and sadly, a lot of them were unable to get out of their own way.

I learned not to fight the facts of my cases. I chose to work honestly and with passion, and to never lie to a client or the court. I wouldn't

19

try to convince the judge that my version of the facts was the correct one. I wouldn't push my version inside the court, and push my clients outside. Those years of lawyering in San Diego were exhilarating, frustrating, engaging, and ultimately the most satisfying work I've ever done.

After thirteen years, however, I had to leave. I had just gotten married, we got a new home in Los Angeles, and I got a new job. Through another set of lucky circumstances, I was appointed a Juvenile Court Referee, which was fine with me. A referee is the same as a judge, a subordinate judicial officer placed on the bench usually for one area of law only.

Being on the bench was a revelation for me. It took me several months to fully adjust to my new role in the court. To go from zealous advocate as a lawyer to neutral fact finder as a bench officer, and make a decision. A lawyer represents one client zealously and presents a set of facts to support that client. A judge listens to all sides, with dispassion and without bias. If there is a jury, the jury will decide which facts rule. If there is not a jury, the judge decides and renders an opinion in Juvie. As a judge, I was still lawyering in my head. I saw substandard lawyering, mistakes being made, a lack of trial preparation, and confusion about the simplest evidence rules.

I often thought, "How did this person ever pass the bar?"

I kept the internal eyerolls to myself. I longed to help any hapless lawyer, regardless of their side. I sometimes betrayed my thinking by asking too many questions. I thought I was being neutral, but my newness showed. After a few months, however, with support and guidance from fellow bench officers, and experience, I learned to let the law speak through me. My love for the work informed my decisions and allowed me to give people a break if I could. My job was not to place the children somewhere specific, or to pick sides, but to place them somewhere safe and loving. Somewhere stable. Somewhere called home.

Eventually, after some time, I was asked to both advise and train new judges. They came and observed or spent time being trained one on one. Then I was asked to teach at Judicial College. To teach new law to new judges was always exciting. Trying to explain the difference between lawyering and judging was something else. I told them to be who they are as people first. If you try to become some other idea of yourself, you will get an ulcer.

I often ended my classes with this axiom, "Be kind, be respectful, don't take sides, and remember it is your court, and your reputation. If you don't love it more than any other job you've ever had, then step down."

Thirty some years later, I am retired and sitting as needed on assignment. I am welcomed back to that wonderful group who are dedicated to the work of helping to repair the world, one family at a time.

8

A Day in the Life of My Courtroom

In California, all juvenile cases are confidential. Outsiders not related to the specific case can only be in the courtroom at the discretion of the bench officer. The only exception was when I hosted social work students and new judges.

Dear reader, I want you to have the same experience as those kids had. So, let me take you through a day in Los Angeles Children's Court, the largest in our country.

When you walk into the Los Angeles County Juvenile Court building and pass security, you will be comforted by a huge wall of children's drawings as you head to the elevator. From there, you will get off at the fourth floor and see a round, colorful waiting area, with small tables and chairs for arts and crafts with the children, benches, and televisions. On the wall, there is a small map and directions for entering your courtroom

Since you have already been cleared by me, check in with the bailiff before taking a seat on the back bench.

We have forty cases on today, several trials, and three new detentions. Detentions are the first hearing for the family. The children have just been removed and are in foster care or with a relative, or they have been allowed to stay home with charges pending.

These kinds of hearings are emotional, with their mix of important legal findings and decisions about where the children will be for the foreseeable future. It is the first meeting the clients have with their own lawyers, one for each mom, one for each legal father, one for all the children, unless there is a conflict among the children. If so, each child gets an attorney. As you can see, the courtroom is getting crowded now. Hundreds of people are waiting, all wanting to be heard. We know. But each family deserves my complete attention. I refuse to rush through the hearings. Luckily, there are usually several easy items, adoptions pending, perhaps some AWOL kids (kids on the run) review hearings for our kids who are in permanent placements. For our foster kids, we check on their health and education, and hope the news is good.

Outside the courtroom, down in the basement, there is a huge room with amenities for children four-years-old and up. Televisions, games, coloring books, an Etch A Sketch, tutors, and breakfast and lunch are provided, for up to around 120 children. Every day. We call that room "shelter care" as it is also the place where removed children can visit their parents and their siblings. They hang out down there until they are brought up to the court when their cases are called.

We also have jail cells for parents in local and state custody who are brought to court. It must be hard for these parents and children to be so close to each other, yet so far. But in a lot of instances, this is for the best.

As you sit in the back, you'll see lawyers running in and out, paperwork being generated, families entering, relatives sitting next to each other on the back bench. Please don't repeat what they are saying! Either I won't be happy, or the parents won't be happy. Just keep what you hear to yourself, please!

Back to the formal process of a first hearing, also called the initial hearing, detention hearing, or arraignment: the parents are provided with a copy of the petition and the accompanying report which states the charges against them. We determine mailing addresses and go over Native American affiliation, which could change the direction of the case. We determine which legal category fathers fit in. With the changes in the law, we now could have a question of legal mothers also, but that is rare. Natural children, adopted children, one-parent children, two-parent children, three-parent children, and every combination you can think of.

Hey, you! Stop talking back there. I know you are astonished at this so far, but wait one minute and there will be more to absorb. If you talk, you will miss something important.

Now, at every subsequent hearing, the same scenario happens. The lawyers argue for the return of the children, or set the matter for trial. I leave the children home, or return them, or keep them out of the home of one or both parents. I make orders for programs or reiterate or modify the original programs that the parents must substantially complete to keep everyone on track or return. If we are at the end of the reunification period, I will stop provision of services, and set the case for permanency for the children.

You are getting the idea. Every hearing is about three things:

1. Is the parent prepared to have the children back at home?
2. Are the children all right where they are?
3. What comes next for the children? What is the plan?

There's more, of course. So much more! But for today, let's skip the motions, the emergency walk-on requests—vacation approvals, warrants for kids, and visitation problems—the special hearings, the eighteen- to twenty-one-year-olds, the parents with long-term prison sentences, you've had enough.

At this point, you have seen the best of us, the worst of us, and above all, the humanity of us. Thank you for coming. Please leave quietly.

A photograph of a child's Etch A Sketch in the courtroom basement. Angela, age seven, drew this while waiting for her hearing.

9

The Personality of the Judge
Sets the Tone of a Courtroom

There is a certain personality profile for dependency judges. Where I worked, I saw almost right away that we were all different in life, experience, age, and ethnicity. Some of us were Type A hypers, some Type B mellows. In fact, we ran the gamut. Some of us had been through our own personal tragedies, some of us were just starting out on the bench, with little, if any, hardships. What did we all have in common? We understand that people screw up. Sometimes they do really bad things. There are those who may not want to change no matter what we say or what life throws at them. But everyone is redeemable. Everyone deserves the right to try.

I get that the Welfare and Institutions Code that drives us is complex and, to some, completely unintelligible. I am never just a judge. I need to be able to go to psychology, to sociology, to medicine, to addiction specialists, to housing authorities, and orchestrate that symphony with everything I have with every case, every day. Most judges are as far from "just a judge" as one can be. The definition of a judge is one who interprets the law. Period. Both sides argue, and either I or a jury decides who argued better. I am not dealing with widgets, or the transfer of money from one large corporation to another. Juvenile law is a calling. It uses everything you've got and more.

I compare my time on the bench to a molten lava chocolate cake. Crusty on the outside, and ooey-gooey on the inside. I am required to uphold, and I agree with, the proposition that the children come first. No matter what. First, protect them. But, to protect the children, I make decisions that are heartbreaking. I break up families, separate children from parents they love and siblings they have sometimes been raising. Foster homes do not always take an entire family of children, and Los Angeles is huge. The children can have different fathers, or mothers, who are available to take custody, sometimes for the first time, and sometimes from different cities or states. Grandparents raise children at a time when they are ready to relax and move on to a gentler time of life, and sometimes they cannot cope with the traumatized children they inherit.

I must balance the needs of the families who want to reunify with the separate obligation we owe to the safety of the children and their outcomes. We want their lives to be better when they leave our system than when they entered. We are doing a lousy job of it, and I spend hours trying to get services that fit the needs of these families.

I know what we need. I've always known what we need, even on my first day on the bench. I started my career as a lawyer in San Diego. After ten years, I transferred to the monolith that is Los Angeles Juvenile Court. A few months later, I was offered my own full-time court, an honor I was thrilled to accept.

I got excited when I ordered my new robe! Then I got my scripts ready to go! When court was called to order, there I was, ready for action and filled with new ideas for how successful my court was going to be. I had lots of plans and chutzpah to back it up!

You know that saying "God laughs while you're busy making plans?" Well, I did not know my staff were lawyers who had all worked together for years. When I called the first case and the family entered the courtroom, immediately there was a verbal argument between the mother's attorney and the county counsel who represented the Department of Children and Family Services. I listened, then watched with jaw agape as the mom's attorney hit the county counsel's shoulder. He shoved back, and in seconds they were punching each other across the floor. I didn't know whether to laugh or cry, but if I didn't take command soon, I would lose all control of my courtroom like a substitute teacher.

I banged my gavel. "Hey! You two! Knock it off!" I roared.

With all eyes on me, I knew I had to set the tone. So I did.

"I will not tolerate this kind of behavior from anyone! Understand!?!"

These families have seen enough violence in their lives. The last place they should see it is in the courtroom! We are not only entrusted with decisions that will affect families, but we need to be civil. How can we admonish families for their behaviors if we can't even manage our own at work?

The rest of that day went smoothly, as did the rest of my time on the bench. Word must've gotten around about my tolerance level.

10

Kavod Ha Bri'ot and Tzedek Tzedek Tirot

I'm not very Jewish because I don't keep kosher. I also don't read the Talmud, and I don't, well, I don't do much of anything. But I was raised Jewish, and that stays with you always. I get myself to the nearest temple for Rosh Hashanah, and Yom Kippur, and I still fast, even though I am past the age of having to, and into the age of may.

There are certain precepts a religious person is raised with, and lives by. A certain worldview, and a sense of right and wrong. We surely don't agree on what those are, but hope one covers all bases such as "Thou shalt not kill."

We are living in a time, and probably always have, where killing others who do not agree with you, is somehow justified. In some instances, it may, in fact, be considered heroic. And confusion reigns when someone universally acknowledged as evil is killed to stop the killing of others. So this philosophical discussion continues. "Black Lives Matter." "The seventy virgins in Paradise." Christian martyrs, and the Crusades. On and on.

What is almost never talked about is the killing of the soul that happens to abused children. We see the physical manifestations when we see the children in the refugee camps, and starving in their villages. What we don't see is the toll on the spirit. On the psyche. On the sense of possibility all children should have.

In Judaism, there are many precepts. I'm sure you all have them too. Two of them have resonated with me, in my role as a juvenile court bench officer.

Kavod Ha Bri'ot means we must ensure the respect and dignity of all human beings. All. Which means not just the ones like me. Not just the Jewish ones, the white ones, the financially okay ones, the educated ones, but all life. This includes the hapless, the poor, even the venal souls who wash up on the shores of my court. It means I cannot assume they do not know how to live, or have no dreams. It means I must help them, parents and children, picture a better life. It means I must try to help them get there. I often fail to speak with a soothing temperament, but my position is that I am there to tell the truth. To tell them what needs to be done, to tell them I will help them get there, and the consequences of failure. They know I mean it, and that I do not talk down to anyone.

Like me or not, I try to speak to the humanity in us all.

Tzedek Tirot is the pursuit of justice. This is the corollary of the first idea on how to treat humanity. It means we act always in a manner predicated on right and wrong. This is where I may not always act in a manner consistent with dignity and respect. Sometimes I just have to let loose on those who hurt children, be it parents, foster parents, or social workers. My temper, which is unfortunately legendary, just erupts when the children get ignored because of laziness on the part of the system, or avarice or worse from foster parents, or parents who repeat awful behaviors over and over and over.

So, who gets dignity and respect? Everyone. Parents and children alike. Is there an exception? Yes. Because first we respect the children. Then we get them justice. So the Kavod Ha Bri'ot and Tzedek Tirot are my guiding principles when it comes to how I rule the courtroom.

Where are yours?

11

Pretending to Be Jewish

Over the years, I've seen my share of parents who are not exactly mentally ill. They are not exactly developmentally delayed. They're just...off. March to a different drummer. Elevator doesn't go to the penthouse. One sandwich shy of a picnic.

In other words, these parents I see in Juvie have a different worldview than the mainstream. Some of them are fairly harmless, needing a fine-tuning by caring professionals to guide them into better choices. I have huge sympathy for these sad folks. But I cannot let that sympathy get in the way of protecting their children from them. And out there on the borderline is not always a safe place for them. Nearly every day these parents get into confrontations with any form of authority.

They are stopped by police with the tailgate out, and respond by taking on the officer. School is a regular battleground, especially if the child has special needs. These parents do not believe in special needs, they like their children just the way they are, and expect us to do the same. We are all to bend to their worldview. Eventually, finally, something snaps, a teacher has had it, or the police are called one more time—and a petition is filed.

I know how to deal with obvious behaviors and scenes that put children at risk. I separate out the act from the person, make it clear what the boundaries and expectations are, and hope they are met. If they are not, I give them fair warning of the consequence and make sure I never make a threat or promise I can't fulfill.

But with the seriously weird, there are no boundaries. Their children are loved, fed, clothed, and, mostly, not abused in the way we normally define abuse. They simply cannot navigate those pesky rules we call civilization. Scenes in public do not faze them, even if the children are present. They are usually banned at the kids' schools. Doctors try in vain to explain what may be needed.

Here is an example that comes to mind. There was a father I'll call "Larry." Larry had two little girls, twins, by surrogate. Mom was not in the picture at all, having given up her rights at birth. At least, that's what Larry said. One of the girls, age seven, was having meltdowns at school, was disruptive, and clearly needed some intervention. Larry disagreed to such a degree, over the course of the year, that the school called the Department. Larry came in with a belligerent attitude, of course, and with no ability to settle down and listen. I sighed. I already knew where this was going. He would want to change lawyers, he would want to get rid of social workers, he would write to the President of the United States regularly. In his effort to find some way in, I noticed Larry was wearing a yarmulke one day. I asked him if he were Jewish, and whether or not he wanted the girls to live in a Jewish foster home. I also asked him if he observed any dietary restrictions. He said yes to both questions, and I knew that giving him some control in this situation might calm him down. I told him that even if we could not find a specific foster home, we could send his list of dietary dos and don'ts to the foster home where the girls would live.

I asked Larry to meet with their social worker and the school, on neutral ground, and if they came to some understanding, I would revisit the return of his girls to him at the jurisdiction hearing in three weeks.

Three weeks later, the girls had been moved twice due to his inappropriate racist remarks to the foster mother. He also had not met with the school. Larry had insulted the social worker with more racist remarks, and she wanted to be taken off the case. Larry's girls were complaining that the other kids in their foster home had pizza, and they had to have some special food that they hated. They also wanted pizza! Susie, the child with the major problems, had to be moved again, but her sister, Claire, was doing well in the second foster home. I made the difficult decision to separate the girls, as it was clear they weren't going home. Larry set the matter for trial, asking for a new lawyer, which I did not grant. Not yet. These clients, I know from my own practice, called their lawyer multiple times daily, for the same reason, and with the same results. Everything was also urgent and they wanted all their needs met now! Now! Now! Now!

I reluctantly took jurisdiction over this case. I say that because fundamentally Larry was not going to change even though he and his children loved each other dearly. All I could do was try to change some small behaviors, one at a time. I sent the girls to therapy. I ordered that Susie take the medication the doctor had ordered, which was against her dad's wishes. And, finally, I ordered Larry to not say anything racist to anyone for the next three months. I had to spell out what constituted racist comments because, in Larry's mind, he was clear that he liked these people and he was just telling it like it was.

Oh yeah, Larry also suddenly stopped wearing his yarmulke. Hmmm.

I had asked Larry about his yarmulke, and in return, I got some vague answer. Hmmm. Pizza for the girls. Hmmm. Surprisingly enough, Larry's social worker (who was Jewish) had found family in another state. Larry's social worker wrote down the conversation in his court report, and this was what was said.

Social worker to sister-in-law, "Do you know a man named Larry Schultz?"

Sister-in-law said, "What did he do now?"

The social worker explained that the children were in foster care, and wondered if she and Larry's brother were interested in having them. She politely declined, saying the less she saw of him, the better.

"By the way," sister-in-law said, "Do you know that 'Larry' is not his real name. He is the half-brother to my husband, which means he is Hispanic. He was raised Catholic, all through school."

The social worker wrote down that the sister-in-law was as clear as she could be that he was not Jewish, never had been, and finished with one of the best lines I had heard on the bench. This nice Catholic lady ended her remarks in pure Yiddish.

"He is a schmuck* and a putz."**

Luckily, I was reading my reports in the morning, before court, and had time to share this conversation with my closest fellow bench officers. We all just howled with laughter. But I also got an idea on how to maybe reach him.

At the hearing, I asked Larry if he had anyone he trusted and got along with. Anyone at all. He did have one friend. I ordered that friend to come to court. I relieved Larry's long-suffering lawyer, but kept the social worker on the case. The social worker was an observant Jew, and apparently, suffering was not a problem for him. He actually liked Larry, who, astonishingly, was starting to trust him. Still, there were lots of insults, but they were kind of ignored by all of us, including the foster mothers of the girls.

We were, in a way, moving to his worldview. Ignore the insults, see the sweetness underneath. Larry was not really such a schmuck after all.

When Larry's friend came to court, I asked if she would monitor Larry's visits with his daughters, and if she could make sure he went to his therapy. She agreed. I ordered a Tourette's evaluation, and a behavior modification therapist. I was not interested in his past, just in getting him to move forward in a less destructive way. Six months after this latest order, with Tourette's ruled out, Larry was finally getting the hang of it. He got an apartment where the landlord could handle him. School was still a problem, but he was agreeing to his kid's medications and special classes. Eventually, his visits were unmonitored, and the girls were ready to go home. Hurray! We did it!

Six months later, we were out of their lives. Larry had modified a bit, enough to get by. We had worked with his support system to keep him on track. We had all learned a bit about managing those "others" that we don't want to deal with.

Now, did I ever tell you about the mom in another case who testified wearing pink footie pajamas and a tiara?

*Jerk
**Jerk

12

Lucy

When I met Lucy, she had her fourth child removed from her custody. Standing in front of me, she was pregnant with her fifth. One of her children died. Another was adopted out. One was with Lucy's mother. Another one was with his father's family. Lucy couldn't care for the child in her womb because, when I met Lucy, she was in Juvenile Hall. She had been sent there for selling and using drugs. She was only seventeen-years-old.

How did we get here? How exactly did Lucy fall through the cracks so many times? Why didn't our services work each and every time we pulled one of her children? She was the very poster child for children having children.

In spite of her poor life choices, I really liked Lucy. These kinds of stories are daily fodder for me, so I was not even shocked. After all, she wasn't raped, and none of the children were fathered by a relative of hers.

We can be cynical and laugh about the shallow end of the gene pool, but what happens in Juvie impacts every other system in America. It impacts the criminal justice system, welfare, housing, schools, the economy, children's rights, and the fundamental right to parent. We need taxpayers, not tax burdens. We need kids in school, healthy and there to learn.

Life here in Juvie is devalued. Our job is to value it again. We see the face of poverty and despair, and it has a name—Lucy. The idea that Lucy lives a life of poverty, want, and deprivation, yet does not realize that she is continuing the cycle of trauma by having more and more children enter the system, is amazing to me. There is a sense of hopelessness, mixed with a sense of entitlement and blame. This is society's fault, and these young women, girls, believe they can do what they want, and we should be responsible after that.

The topic of reproductive rights arguments for abortion and preventative birth control is really not discussed. I bring it up, carefully, and with as much tact as I can to girls like Lucy.

"Perhaps you might consider getting these kids back before you have another," is as far as I am willing to go. And I think even that may be frowned upon us inappropriate. I am far more specific with my teens, but it's way too late for Lucy.

Most of my young women do not think about pregnancy. Not before, not during, not after. They mostly do not get pregnant specifically for the welfare money, but take it when it comes. They know they should not drink or take drugs during pregnancy, but they do it anyway. Then they lie about it. I'd ask girls like Lucy, "How did drugs get into the baby's system?" I'd get the same variation of answers from different young women.

"Someone put it in my soda."

"I inhaled it from the air at the party I attended."

"Oral sex."

"I don't know."

You could number the excuses. On occasion, we'll get a new one.

"My acrylic nails got into the baby's bloodstream."

If you have not thought about mandatory sterilization in your life, you have not been exposed to Juvie. I have seen parents who should not be given a chia pet. Some families should stop procreating. Just stop. From the great-grandparents who had lost their children through the grandparents who had lost their children to the parents who had lost their children, to the children who had lost their children. I had one mother who had lost child after child to drugs. Adoption after adoption. I would see her each year with another baby, each time with an unknown father. I would ask her what happened, and she finally said to me, "You know me, I just screwed up."

I did know her, and I felt not anger, but deep despair. I simply could not let her give up. So, we started again, baby number I can't remember, and that time, yes that time, it took. We worked together, me as a cheerleader for her small steps to sobriety. I kept telling her she could do it, and that last time, she did!

Returning her child to her was one of my good days. Terminating court jurisdiction six months later was one of my greatest days. She never came back. I wished her and her child the very best and hoped to never see them again.

I always felt that each child was an opportunity for a new start, even if some part of me said, "Yeah, sure." I had hoped each time, and offered services when it was legal to do so. California has tightened its belt with regard to providing services for baby after baby. I would have a hard time today doing anything other than going directly to adoption for that third, or fourth, or twelfth child.

But there were always ways, motions that could be brought, and heard, that allowed me to give that one last chance. That possible miracle.

You may be asking yourself why I would even bother. These women should not be parents. Because children want to be with their mothers, and grandmothers, and great-grandmothers. Because all statistics show that children need to know who they are and where they come from. Finally, because children who have children eventually grow up, and sometimes when they grow up, they actually grow up. And this cycle stops.

Finally.

13

We All Need the Voice of Love

I have cassette tapes. Also, vinyl, and CDs. That's it. No music through any machine. My tapes go back to the fifties, vinyl to the twenties, and my CDs are relatively new. My favorite tapes are ones made for me by my friends and family, all customized by playing different tracks and recording them. For example, the tape my husband made of all my favorite high school songs. My son once gave me all of the songs Billie Holiday, Lady Day, recorded in 1944, my birth year. But the ones that I value above all are the ones my father painstakingly made for me before he died. Miriam Makeba on one side, Odetta on the other. Louis Prima and Keely Smith, with Sam Butera and the Witnesses as the band. Benny Goodman.

Every morning, I get to court at 5:30 a.m. I need to have a few hours to myself to read all my reports and plan my day. I prepare questions, that the reports do not answer, so that I can get the information before I call the case. I usually talk to a colleague, either on the phone or just dropping by my chambers. While I prepare the day, I also play my tapes.

One morning, very early, I had my Louis Prima tape on. I was rocking to "Just a Gigolo" when the song ended. Normally, I would have turned the tape over, but I was in the middle of reading a report. So I left the tape to run out. I was reading in silence when all of a sudden, I heard my dad's voice. He was telling me how much he loved me, and how much he knew I would love this tape. His voice got me to stop reading. I looked up from the report and though my chambers were empty, I felt my dad's presence with me in that room. He had been gone for about ten or more years at that time. I had completely forgotten that he talked to me on the tapes. He had seen me become a lawyer, but not get to the bench.

My clerk came in a little after I heard my father talk to me. He was there to take files into the courtroom. But there I was, sobbing into those files, hard and loud. My clerk was taken aback, and immediately concerned.

I explained myself as tears ran down my face. "I'm sorry...I just heard the tape my father made for me. He died ten years ago. I forgot he left a message for me on the tape and I just heard."

I got a warm hug in response, which was what I needed in that moment. And then...it was time to move on with our day.

I had the best father. He made me a reader, a thinker, and an independent woman. In his eyes, everything I did was great! He was always so proud of me. While he could be a little too quick to take credit for my every success, he was also there for my failures too. How lucky I was to have such a wonderful dad.

So, how does this story relate to Juvie? There is the obvious need for any child to have at least one voice in their favor. One voice that tells them they are with worthwhile, one voice that tells them they will prevail. One voice to remind us that we are loved. My sister and I didn't have a lot growing up, but we always had enough. Kids, even in the worst circumstances, bloom when they have at least one cheerleader. It could be a family member, a teacher, a family friend, anyone who takes the time to make a child feel special.

And trust me when I say, when children hear the voice of a loved one, whether in their heads or even on a tape, that voice will echo onward in the best possible way.

14

Amy and Deliah

So, I've told you that there are times when people are wondrous to behold. When, after the tenth domestic-violence-fueled-by-drugs-or-alcohol case, a case comes in that makes it all worthwhile again. I call them palate cleansers, a nice break between courses.

I had just finished deciding on the long-term plan for two very disturbed teenagers, who will spend the rest of their lives medicated and housed in facilities, when Amy was strolled into my courtroom. Amy was a six-year-old child who had been left with no parent or guardian. Her father was unknown, her mother had just passed away from cancer, and all other relatives were unknown or uninterested. When Amy's mother got sick, her friend, Deliah, took them both in. Deliah cared for Amy until her mother died.

Amy was a beautiful, delightful child with Down's Syndrome. As Deliah strolled Amy into the courtroom, everyone got a big, bright smile from Amy. Amy was high functioning, able to communicate well, and just a joy to be around. Amy was there in front of me because Deliah wanted to adopt her. As long as Deliah lived and breathed, she would do what she could to prevent Amy from entering foster care. If Amy had entered foster care, she most likely would have been raised in facilities because it is hard to find homes for children with special needs. It gets harder as they grow older.

There was no argument. She cried when I officially started the process, when she knew Amy was not going to be removed from her care. She wasn't the only one.

We deal with every kind of person in Juvie. From the evilest to the most sainted. People who are supposed to be the protectors will instead use, abuse, sell, and neglect their own children. To some people, children are things, only there for the parents' needs. And then there are those people like Deliah who take in broken children and nurture, care for, support, and heal them. Sometimes the saints and sinners are from the same family.

15

Judges Should Play Mahjong on Wednesdays

On the day another one of my Juvie friends retired, I thought more about what it takes to do our job, what qualities one needs to do it well for a long period of time. You need to have compassion, tolerance, some common sense, a good sense of humor, and wonderful colleagues.

I'm not sure in what measure I had the first on the list, but I was blessed with the latter in full measure.

Juvie is an unwanted assignment. Stark, busy, and difficult, it is distasteful to most judges, and they leave as soon as they are allowed. The learning curve is high, as most have not lawyered in the area, and the rewards few. In most courts, collegiality is kept to some formality, from cool nods in the cafeteria, to perhaps warmer conversation and meetings, depending on the personalities in each court. I got lucky. Really lucky.

My friend and fellow judge, Donna, and I started on the same day, two courts apart. As a new transplant from San Diego, I knew no one. On my first day, Donna knocked on the door of my chambers with a cup of tea, and a welcome. On the second day, she had a law question she wanted to run by me. By the end of my first week, morning tea became a ritual, and both of us were being fairly assertive to the point that our discussions became more heated. We could be heard in the judges' hallway. One day there was a knock at the door; it was another judge, wanting us to weigh in on a dilemma she was having. And that's how it started. Soon, our early mornings were full of legal conversations. What fun! Then it got better.

For my fifty-second birthday, in 1996, my husband gave me an antique Mahjong set. Mahjong is a tile-based game from China. Like the westernized Rummy game, Mahjong is a game of skill, strategy, and luck. My husband had heard me talking about playing some thirty years before. I mentioned the game to Donna, and she said she would love to learn. We asked our court friends, and many said yes.

Los Angeles Juvie is the largest juvenile court system in the world. In my time, there were nineteen dependency courts, on three floors. There were twenty-eight delinquency courts regionalized around the county. Many of us were new; some of us had been sitting for years, even before the current building was built. So we were pretty varied in age, ethnicity, gender, and experience. Yet, within weeks, there we were, with our new Mahjong cards, in my chambers playing, laughing, and talking about our morning calendar. Soon, other judges started to bring their lunches into our Wednesday game, and it became the place to gather once a week. We closed the door and spent the lunch hour playing, helping a colleague with a knotty case, talking about the lawyers, and being completely inappropriate with our dark and profane humor. Those game days gave us opportunities to help each other through the day. Legal issues were debated, sometimes heatedly, as the Code book went from hand to hand, until consensus was reached. And the game went on, through it all.

My chambers were a safe place, a place where there were no wrong questions, or answers. We were all there because we wanted to be, and we intended, most of us, to stay. I have never been in such a loving work situation. For almost thirteen years, every Wednesday, the core group came every week; we said goodbye to some, and welcomed others, in a bubble of friendship. We asked each other for help whenever we needed it, but Wednesdays were different. When you feel so supported, you take chances. And give them. The job remains the same, but the payoffs are bigger, as we are braver. Those who came to play Mahjong with me are my closest court friends to this very day.

But Wednesday is gone, and I hear now that people don't get together very much anymore. The new people do not stay, and I mourn the loss. To feel safe and supported in a difficult milieu is not to be taken lightly. Our jobs are heavy, it is important for our hearts to be light. At least once a week.

Wednesday Maj.

16

Elders Can Help the Family Connection Going

It was "Caring Elders Day" at my grandson's middle school. My grandson, Bennet, is in seventh grade. The middle school is in Berkeley, California. Organic. I flew up for this event, honored that my grandson asked for me to come, and because, as my son said, "Mom, you never give up the opportunity to get a sash."

My grandson and I walked to school together, and joined the line of other people with their relatives waiting to check in. There were older brothers and sisters, grandparents, aunts, uncles, and a fair number of parents. We all laughed and talked with each other as our kids squirmed and stepped away. The invitation didn't negate those twelve-year-olds from being embarrassed for being seen with an adult during waking hours.

After we checked in, had our picture taken, and I got my sash, we entered the cafeteria, where a wonderful breakfast was served. After which we proceeded to the auditorium, where we were entertained by the school dance group and the orchestra. Wonderful!

But the best part of the day was accompanying Bennet to his classroom, where we all sat together. The day was spent with the children asking us elders questions about our school days. There were Hispanic relatives who didn't speak English, whose kids translated for them; African-American relatives; white; Indian; and Asian. We were all of a "certain age," with a wild variety of school experiences.

When we were asked what we would've wished to have back then, that our kids have now, most said computers. I had a different answer.

"Diversity," I said.

I then went on to explain that in all my school years, until college, everyone I knew looked like me, talked like me, and acted like me. My grandson had never known a moment in his life without a rich mélange of people in it, kids of every ethnicity, mixed or not. My grandson has friends with parents of mixed ethnicity, same sex or not.

As soon as I said all this, other relatives added their take on the same subject and it got quite lively. We discussed bullying, and prejudice, and the ways "things were back then" to whatever "back then" was as defined for each of us.

After our discussions died down, and the kisses goodbye, we left, and regular school continued.

It was a wonderful day.

Recalling this fond memory of "Caring Elders Day" makes me think about the role elders play in Juvie families. The one thing we look for in Juvie is in fact that caring elder. Elders have a lot to offer their families as they have been on this earth long enough to have seen it all, outside in the world and in their own families. Elders usually have financial stability and wisdom to better know how to handle the challenges their families are in. Someone to connect with that child. Someone to provide some sort of stability in their grandchildren's chaotic worlds. Mostly it's a grandparent in the family who can be a stable force. But it can also be, and has been, older siblings, aunts and uncles. It can be family friends, teachers, Court Appointed Special Advocates (CASA), and sometimes, in a lovely twist, the different father of siblings. While the elder in the family is responsible for the child, we encourage the rehabilitating parent to visit, frequently, and encourage the children when they are there. To read to their children, and, if home visits are allowed, to feed, bathe, and otherwise parent them. All of this needs to be done to keep that connection going.

The elders in the family can help keep the bond between the parent and child. When we all add our hearts, our experiences, our hugs, and our pasts to the present, we add to the continuum of life. To raise healthy, confident children, no matter where they find themselves.

And when all is said and done, it's about love after all.

Me and my grandson, Bennet.

17

We Should Connect with Others
Every Chance We Get

When my daughter, Abby, turned twenty-one, she was doing a year abroad in Bath, England. I took my niece, Jill, with me as a surprise. My daughter and niece were six months apart and very close. We started by flying to Scotland for a week, then we took a train down to England. It was a fun vacation.

So, I was in the train station waiting for the train to Bath; the girls had gone off to do something. I sat next to a woman on a bench and we started to chat. Where are you from, stuff like that.

Then I asked her a question, "I saw these very long-haired animals all over the country. What are they called?"

She thought about it, then said in a very slow and exaggerated manner, "Sheeep."

I looked at her for a minute, then she realized I knew what sheep looked like, and the two of us completely broke down laughing. Stomach hurting laughing. Can't catch your breath laughing. When we finally wiped our eyes and calmed down, she correctly told me about Highland cows, which are small long-haired cows in the pastures of Scotland.

In that moment I thought, wouldn't it be wonderful if we could always handle misunderstandings with shared laughter?

My husband and I were once visiting friends and family in Phoenix. We were told not to miss the Music Museum. It was astonishing. The history of music from its beginnings through film, costume, and instruments orchestrated in amazing small vignettes. One little corner had an homage to Johnny Cash. His guitar, some song lyrics, and a screen. On the screen, on a loop, was an older Johnny, singing on a couch. On the stairs, watching him, was June Carter Cash, his wife of thirty some years. As I stood there, I started to well up, and sniff. All of a sudden a hand reached over from next to me, handing me a tissue. A perfect stranger stood next to me and we sniffed together for a minute or two, before we ended up giving each other a smile and a hug.

And it was in that moment that I thought, wouldn't it be wonderful if we could always have a tissue to give a person in need?

We can. We can open our hearts. We can accept our kids with troubling behavior, with different language abilities, with needs we don't understand.

I've always used humor in my courtroom. Always made light of truth to reach families who needed to hear it. So can you. And if there is some way in your life you can help someone else, known or not, take it.

It will be a wonderful experience.

18

Grandma Gets a Tattoo

So, my sixty-fifth birthday was fast approaching, and I was feeling it. Usually, I can't be bothered with my age. I was doing a job I love, had a wonderful family life, friends, and lots of activities. But still...I was feeling my age.

Craig and I were having brunch on the boardwalk in Venice, California with a friend. After brunch, we took a walk to enjoy the beautiful day. As we walked, we people watched. Venice is a part of California that has decided that the sixties was a great time, and there was no reason to leave it.

We walked along looking at the various booths set up selling everything "groovy" and psychedelic. It was fun. As we passed the tattoo parlor, one of several, I made up my mind. It was time to shake things up! In my line of work, I have had many conversations about body work and piercings with my court kids. We have debated how many and where, as they cannot get tattoos without my permission, unless they are with a parent.

I have often discussed the ramifications of getting a skull tattoo on your future job prospects. The inconvenience of one girl's name on the arm, when that girl is gone, and the new girl isn't ready to ignore it. Then there are the piercings on the face, and elsewhere. And I have ordered funds for removal as the first thrill faded and a tattoo's reality set in.

However, my kids didn't have a lot of ability to show who they were. To differentiate themselves by clothes or fashion. There was very little money to experiment. So I was loathe to say no to seventeen-

and-eighteen-year-olds. Especially if there was not a man or woman parent in Juvie who was not inked. One enterprising and angry mother had "F--- the Social Worker" emblazoned on her upper chest for all to see, especially her social worker. The men wore ink from shaved head to colored sleeves, legs, and hands. Every available space was covered in thoughts and politics. Kids' names and ages, pictures of political figures, religious symbolism were proudly displayed. So, in that milieu, it was hard to say no, especially if the seventeen- and eighteen-year-olds had earned the money. Usually, there is a compromise, in that I allowed the least they would accept, and they kept the piercings to an absolute minimum.

And so there I was, on a bright, sunny day on the Venice boardwalk, ripening into those golden years, and feeling just like my kids do. Rebellious, itching to shout that I am a person, unique.

The young man who worked at the tattoo parlor politely asked me if he could help me.

"Yes. I want a tattoo," I said.

The young man laughed.

I looked at him, serious as could be. "I mean it."

The facial expression on the young man's face suddenly changed. He got very excited.

"Awesome!" he said. "You will be my first *abuela.*"*

As I got situated, I thought I wasn't his first grandmother. I was just probably the first grandmother in there who looked like a grandmother. Anyway, I told him what I wanted, and drew it out.

"I want it simple, classy."

The young man pulled out a chaise from the back so I didn't have to sit in a regular chair. Did I mention I feel faint at the sight of the flu shot needle? Nuts, you say? Oh yes.

My husband held my hand, and off we went. It didn't take long, it didn't hurt, and it looked great. It is a simple ankle bracelet with a small purple flower. It healed perfectly.

So, my court kids and I have a little something in common now. I have some idea of why people want this, and some "street cred" to boot!

*Translation "grandmother."

19

LGTBQIA2S+

LGBTQIA2S+. Lesbian, Gay, Bisexual, Transgender, Queer, Intersex, Asexual, Two-Spirit and the plus sign (+) signifies the inclusion of additional identities or orientations. These are the hotbed issues. I cannot open a magazine or watch a television program that does not in some way cite this issue. Programs that have added that one Black character, then the one Latin character, preferably a female, now have that one LGBTQIA2S+ character.

Will and Grace, a popular television show in the 1990s, dealt with the day-to-day lives of people who happened to be gay. Ellen stopped the presses with her on-air pronouncement of being a lesbian. The man who won the decathlon in the Olympics was now a transwoman. Lots of talk, lots of opinions. Matthew Shepard, a twenty-one-year-old student at the University of Wyoming, was brutally tied to a fence and killed for being gay, an event that made national news and continues to haunt. How can you be killed for what you are? Now, take that prejudice and apply it to young, teenaged foster children.

If ever there was a wit's end group in a wit's end job, these are gay kids in foster care. Mostly, they are in the system because they have been rejected for religious and other reasons by the families of origin. They come into my court already battered, and trying to negotiate a system not geared to their special need to feel special. To just live, to decide, to seek. I am aware that their abuse is not apparent on the outside. I deal all day with kids who have been bruised in calculable ways. Physical abuse, sexual abuse, neglect were all able to be charted by doctors, dentists, teachers. But the harm to a child, already confused and questioning, by rejecting him or her because of something which cannot be changed, like red hair or blue eyes, is incalculable.

LGBTQIA2S+ kids are angry. They are scared, and rough. There are not enough beds to go around, as many foster homes do not want to mix gay kids with straight kids. I try to ignore the obvious, and deal with them as children, and only children. I cannot. The way they look, the way they behave, the way they talk all provide fodder for how they are treated in school, home, community.

This is the twenty-first century, you say. One's private life should be private, and personal choices not weighed more than personal achievement. You would be wrong.

These kids are still a problem for society. Boys that lisp, or prance, girls with shaved heads and combat boots continue to frustrate the norm. And transgender, or almost transgender, kids continue to confound. I pulled out my hair trying to find a place for them to live first. School was a nightmare. Medical needs were major. And while most of these kids were simply trying to live a meaningful and real life, many were beyond frustrating to handle.

Take Ernest/Lori. He was born a boy to a religious Filipino family. When he came to me, he was incorrigible, refusing to go to school or follow the rules of the house. He was fourteen. His mother, in spite of her religious beliefs, loved her child, and never gave up on him. She was at every hearing, hoping he would choose to return home, and give up the very risky lifestyle he was living as a girl, dressing as a girl, while engaging in high-risk sex on the streets and using drugs. He refused any help, and as time went on, was arrested more and more frequently. Once Ernest identified as a female named Lori, had long hair, painted long nails, and female clothing, it was hard to know which jail to put her in? What home would take her? I despaired. I lectured. I begged. I told her that I strongly believe she would be dead by eighteen. She laughed, and refused to compromise in any way. She ran away from any placement, jumped out of the social workers' cars on the way to placements. At eighteen, she was gone. I terminated jurisdiction, with a prayer for her safety, not believing it for one minute.

Fast forward to the opposite side of the coin. On adoption days, I am always aware and grateful that the families who take our hardest babies to care for are frequently gay and lesbian. Healthy, successful, loving families, willing to take children of any ethnicity, or gender and provide them with a stable home.

When acceptance and love are given to a child, acceptance and love are what you get back. Pass it on. They do.

20

Teenage Girls

One morning I heard twenty cases, and while some were easier than others, I was in need of a break. I needed those fifteen minutes in the morning to decompress, have a cold drink, and just get off the bench. I answered e-mails, got telephone messages, or talked to a colleague. After fifteen minutes, I was ready to tackle the rest of the morning, but then...

Veronica came into my courtroom. She was my typical teenage girl, stuck in a foster home she didn't like, in an area she did not like, going to a school she did not like, and with other kids she...you get the picture. I wasn't sure if she was pregnant. In dealing with this case, I sighed. Sometimes I sighed out loud. Once I even said "whatever" out loud. But, you see, this was why I was there. Giving babies a loving home was not the hardest thing in the world to do, usually. Even our three- to six-year-olds come out all right, mostly. Over six-years-old, we hoped for good relatives or permanent foster homes. But our teens were always in for a rough ride. Even if we found good relatives, these kids wear them out. Teens test the adults in their lives.

Will you still love me if I do this? How about this? Or this?

We talk to them until we're blue in the face, but it's all in vain.

Teenagers like Veronica won't go to school. They won't go to therapy. They use foster placements like Airbnbs to be dropped in, shower, sleep, then run away again.

The worst is that oftentimes the human traffickers that prey on these teens' vulnerabilities get to them first, and offer better than what we can. At least that is what teens like Veronica say. Freedom is offered to them. Material possessions are offered. And these kids, boys and girls, want both and they want them now. Instant gratification.

Studies show that children have stopped living at the time of their trauma. They are the age that trauma occurred. So, if they were at an early age, they throw tantrums. Maybe they don't get down on the floor and kick their feet, but pretty close. The older trauma-infused will hide, even in plain sight. Hair covering the face, head down, their answers are short and voices low.

I try to find something nice to say. "Purple hair looks good on you," I said, and I meant it. Sometimes I get a smile or two, and try to leverage that into some conversation.

"Any new friends at school?"

"Tell me one class you like."

I move into hopes, dreams, maybe ask how can I help? But the deeper I try to delve, the faster the walls go up. Arms get crossed. Answers become more belligerent. I have had kids get up and walk out, yelling at me all the way.

These kids want what they want and they want it now! I have tried to explain why they cannot go home for the tenth time. Why they cannot return to grandma, who has asked for their removal yet again. Their belongings, as they move from foster home to foster home, to group home, are in black garbage bags.

A life in a black plastic garbage bag. Heartbreaking.

So I grit my teeth. I try again to find something, anything, to build a bridge, to engage them, to show them how desperately I want to help make their individual lives better. But their trauma gets in the way. They cannot concentrate, or make long-range decisions. They trust no one, at least no one in the system.

They mostly don't believe me when I say I want to help. But sometimes they do. And sometimes I get through, and sometimes what I say I want to do, I actually get the system to do. Some have had a loving adult at some point, even if gone now, and have a modicum of trust. You can't lie or promise.

These teens will soon become adults. It's important to show them that we care. Otherwise, their children may end up in my courtroom.

None of us wants that.

Teenage girls are sometimes brought in by their group home, sometimes by probation, much more rarely by a foster parent or relative. They are the vehement, vociferous viragos of Juvie. The teenage girls who Don't. Want. To. Hear. It.

I get that we are messing with their lives. I get that they do not want to be anywhere they are, not in court, not in the group home, not with that foster parent, not in their own skin. They are fourteen, fifteen, sixteen, seventeen, those wonderful ages already hormonally crazy for any child.

Foster teenagers have been through it all, and then some. They have seen it all, and then some. They have rousted parents out of drug-induced comas, taken care of their siblings for years, and seen their families collapse under the weight of their dysfunction.

And they are mad. Anger plus frustration plus fear equals mad. They are not completely able to make sane and reasoned decisions. So they make really bad ones. Over and over. No school, bad men, easy victims of trafficking. They say they like having sex, they were doing it anyway so they might as well get paid. Pregnancy happens. Again. They don't get to keep their babies, as they stay out all night with them, partying with their friends.

Teenage boys have their own agendas, but mostly they either end up in delinquency or harm themselves. The girls are more spectacular. They are fighting for their lives, and I am just one more roadblock.

I tell them I can help. They cross their arms and glare. I ask what they are interested in so as to formulate a plan. They say nothing interests them, except being allowed to live with the boyfriend I already found unacceptable.

They run, we find them, they run again. They get arrested for prostitution, and we locked them up for a short time. Once free, they run again. We have finally become enlightened enough to realize they are also victims, and locking them up is counter-intuitive to their needs. But we cannot meet their needs if they won't let us help them.

Impasse. Standstill. When they are in court, it is a tornado of yelling, leaving, mute disrespect. What am I to them? More system. More useless system. Did we save their siblings? Did we straighten out their parents?

I scramble to find something to say in those moments when I'm facing a teenage girl. To reach in and grab that scared little kid inside of them. I could hardly ever get past the secondary personality, the one with the thick shell. But still I tried. Was there a compromise? Was there anything we could agree on? Could they meet me any of the way, even if not half?

In one hearing, there was a young woman brought in by probation. She had been arrested, and was waiting for her delinquency case to be heard at a later time. I thought how beautiful she was, and how withdrawn. She was turned away from me, to show her disdain. I, without thinking, said something to her.

"You know, orange is not a good color for you."

I was commenting on her jail coveralls. This beautiful teenaged girl turned to look at me, and started to laugh. Miracle!

"So, what can we do to keep you out of that color going forward?" I asked her. From there, a small dialogue happened, and when she left, I thought, who knew? Who knew a simple statement without any serious judgment and deep introspection would actually work better than all the psychological stuff?

Don't get me wrong, the psychological stuff is always needed, but it was easier to get agreement with laughter than with a frown.

I thought to try that method again in my future dealings with teenagers. If only I had thought to do that earlier!

21

I Will Always Follow the Law, But There Was One Day...

There is an old lawyer trick, "There was no murder here. If you all look at the back of the courtroom, the supposed victim will walk into the courtroom." All eyes will turn to the back of the courtroom. Except one set of eyes. The murderer's, who knows the victim will not appear. In juvenile court, the children always look.

I am a retired juvenile court bench officer. I was on the bench for seventeen years. Before that, I was an attorney for ten years. In 2007, I was named California Juvenile Court Judge of the year. Working with children was not the easiest way to spend one's time, but the day I stepped into juvenile court, I was home.

Some days are better than others. The best part of the day is when I can return a child back home to parents who, with little money, little education, and lots of work, transformed their lives to provide a better life for their children. Finalizing an adoption of a child who's endured years of abuse is another great day. Reuniting siblings who have long been separated is as rewarding as it gets.

The kids were nine, eight, seven, six, and five. Girl, boy, boy, boy, girl. The youngest, Dinah, still sucked her thumb in court. They were in five foster homes, having been removed from the mother for her drug use. As is not unusual in these cases, we did not have an identifiable father. The five men the mother named all had unknown whereabouts. In the eight years I had this case, we never found one father. All five kids were special needs, both educationally and emotionally. They were not bonded to each other, and did not care if they saw each other. The oldest girl and the boys went from foster home to foster home. I saw them every six months, as the law prescribed, and if their behavior warranted more intervention, which it often did, I'd try to stabilize their placement or add more services. Their mother disappeared soon after the kids were taken into foster care, and never once attempted to make contact with them at all.

There are two main goals in Juvie, working side by side. The first is to return children to their home of origin, or a permanent home, within eighteen months of the original removal. The second is to acknowledge that some children will never have a permanent home, and they are ours to raise. I raised hundreds of children, from babies to emancipation, and my goal was to make sure they got exactly what I would want for my own natural children in these circumstances. I fought long and hard for a good education, good therapy, activities to enrich and sustain, and help formulate a plan for passage from our system to independence. I was not as successful as I wanted to be.

The Los Angeles children's court is a model for all children's courts. It was designed for kids, from the arts programs in their waiting rooms, to the huge "shelter care" room on the bottom floor, which houses, feeds, educates, and cares for up to a hundred kids every day. From age four to age twenty, they are brought from all parts of Los Angeles County to the court. They are delivered to our courtrooms by volunteers, through a special elevator and down the back hall corridors that only the judges can access. Each courtroom has a small waiting area, filled with books and toys, where the children wait to have their cases called. Each and every child looks immediately to the back of the courtroom as they are brought into the courtroom, to see who has come on their behalf. Is Grandma there? An aunt? Mom and Dad? Anyone? For my five kids in the Mitchell family, no one ever came. Until...one day.

I was seeing the kids when my bailiff approached me and told me that the mother was outside. These kids had been in the system for about seven years at that point; the oldest girl had run away and was gone, but the boys, and the youngest child, Dinah, were still with me. Dinah, at fourteen, was still sucking her thumb in court and had many problems, but the boys were doing extremely well. Each one was in a good and stable home, school was going great, and they were cheerful, clean, and charming in court.

I was in a pickle.

Taking a deep breath, I told the bailiff to let her come in. I then told the kids, as gently as I could, that their mother was in court that day, and would be entering the courtroom. They had never had a visit, a call, or a letter from her during their near decade in foster care. We all waited. The door opened, and a woman slithered in. That is the only way to describe this picture. Six feet tall, reed thin, she slowly entered and advanced toward the front court seats. She wore tight black leather pants and a see-through black lace top. Her hair was done, her makeup was perfect, her nails were done, and all the kids went nuts. I stopped the proceedings for them to hug her and kiss her, and Dinah grabbed her hand and would not let go. I called the case, and the lawyers made their appearances. I told the mother how happy I was to see her, and that I hoped she had spent the last several years doing what she needed to reclaim her children.

"Is there anything I can do to help you?" I asked her.

All four children and I waited for her response.

This mother looked straight at me and said, "So, I was told that if I had my children, I am entitled to extra money and not just welfare?"

Someone told her this in the community. There are several financial tiers for foster care, depending on the special needs of the children, and specialized homes get more money.

I had to explain this. "The children were receiving a special rate for specialized services, but a parent would not get that money."

Without looking at or speaking to her children, not even once, she got up, turned around, and slithered right out of the room. The children did not turn to watch her leave. They were watching me become verklempt as they stood still, emotionless.

This is why judges are not permitted to have guns on the bench.

22

Sometimes, It Is the Children
Who Make the Decisions

In my courtroom, there was a small category of cases that were decided almost completely by the children. While the parents' behavior gave rise to the original petition, the children ran the show. I was just along for the ride. The cases were invariably emotional, sometimes bittersweet, sometimes breathtaking in the courage shown by children as young as six or seven.

These children did not want to go home. Ever. They did not want to see their parents. Ever. They absolutely refused to cooperate with any conjoint counseling I ordered. They would, however, go if I said it was a one-time session in order to clear the air with their parents and say goodbye. I always hoped it may have led to some rapprochement, and maybe more sessions. But it rarely did.

There had been cases where the oldest child cared for the younger siblings while also bearing the brunt of their parent's drug use and neglect. Those siblings got taken away and ended up in a safe and stable permanent home while the oldest child was separated from them, living with a relative or in foster care. Usually, in these types of cases, the oldest sibling has had it. Their own life and how to better it has become the priority.

Requests would be made to see siblings and not have to reunify with the parents. After trying everything, and assuring the young person in these situations that one cannot go around, under, or over the problem of one's past—only through it—I often granted the desire and order of no contact with the parents until the girl or boy requested it.

A story that pops in my mind when it comes to children deciding not to live with parents is that of Luca. Luca was a little six-year-old boy, his legs not long enough to even bend over the witness chair, telling the court in a matter-of-fact way about the physical torture his parents put him through. Beatings, burnings, neglect, he recounted it all. We saw the pictures of the burns and bruises, and the condition of the house, but the lawyers had a right to call him as a witness. The parents' attorneys cross-examined him, trying every which way to shake his story, but they were unable to move him one inch. We were in tears at his courage and his strength. In my decision, I lapsed out of judicial restraint to say that these parents should not be allowed to own a Chia Pet, let alone raise children. I then ordered Luca and his sister be placed in a foster home together. I ordered regular visitation, monitored, with the parents. The younger sister went to the monitored visits, but he would not. Luca never returned home. He and his sister ended up being adopted by their loving foster parents.

We know about the molested girls, the ones whose mothers' boyfriends are the molesters, and the mothers either do not believe it, or blame the victim, the child. We know these children will not go back to that home, but it is difficult to help the victim when their siblings are returned. Older boys, who were not at risk, generally wanted to stay out of the fray, and just wanted to go home to their rooms and reunite with their school friends. The other girls, who I believe were at risk, blamed the victim because I would not let them return home so long as the mother protected the molester. So the child, who was a victim of molestation, would lose all support and all family at the same time. These were angry children, and I had to dance pretty fast to try to get through to them. I failed as often as I succeeded. I was so angry for them. I may not work as hard as I should to "fix" the mother. These girls were ripe for being trafficked, runaways, or ending up pregnant. These young, victimized girls were too hurt to move ahead, and too damaged to see family as family.

Then there were the children of mentally ill parents. They negotiated for them as long as they could until they had gotten fed up or lost the never-ending battles that come with dealing with someone who is not mentally well. These children loved their parents, but would drown in their care.

Lisa was eleven when she was living with her mother, Roberta, a paranoid schizophrenic. One day, Roberta was found wandering the streets, completely disoriented.

Roberta loved her daughter with all her heart...when she remembered she had one. Lisa was placed in a foster home with an older foster parent, one who was willing to work with Roberta. Lisa's mother went in and out of her illness over the next two years. Lisa had said pretty early on that she did not want to go home anymore. "Home" was shelters and freeway underpasses. Lisa finally had clean clothes, a bedroom, regular school, and the right to be a child. She asked me if she could be adopted by her foster mother, who wanted her. Lisa asked me to be adopted in court with her mother present. I said yes because her mother was simply never going to be motivated to follow any course of medication or treatment. The adoption took place, but for years after, Roberta kept filing paperwork to regain custody of her child. She would show up at court and ask for hearings which were long over. The adoption was heartbreaking for her, heartwarming for her child, and heart-rendering for me.

In my presence, parents have argued regularly that the children prefer their "nicer" foster homes, the ones with the swimming pools and beautiful bedrooms, as a reason their children do not want to come home. I disagree with these generalizations since I never once saw that.

Finally, there are those children, placed with relatives, who have had it! Simply have had it. As have the relatives. They have enabled, helped, excused their adult children, siblings, cousins for the last time. These children in their relatives' care have sent me letters. Lots of letters.

Here are some letters from a sibling set, Jose and Jenna. Their parents have let them down far too many times to count and they wrote to me about it. They wrote a letter to their mother too.

Dear Your Honor,

Your honor, I am writing this letter because I am asking you to please, please don't let my mom take me away from where I am with my family in LA. Please can you please read this letter and the one I sent to my mom? Thank you for your time.

Sincerely,
Jose

Your Honor,

Please don't move my brother and I. We're happy with my aunt. She takes care of us and she's always been there. Please read the letters I wrote to my mother and father. In those letters, I express myself and how I actually feel. My mother never took care of me and my father never reached out to find me and take care of me. Please, your honor, my brother and I are happy here. This is our family and they'll take care of us and protect us. Please, your honor, don't move us.

Sincerely,
Jenna

Dear the person who gave birth to me,

I am writing this to ask you if you could please stop fighting for us...

Jenna then wrote two pages of her disgust and anger at her mother while emphasizing her love for and safety with her aunt.

And finally, a letter to their mother from Jose.

Dear Mom,

I want you to know that I love you and I will always love you. You will always be my mom, but I want to ask you, please don't take me away. I don't wanna (sic) live with you. I remember when you left that I was sad about it, but now I'm used to living without you, so please, please don't take me. I want to stay here with my Tia and Jenna and dog Pelusa. When you left, we had to give away Tigre and Pookie. I don't want that again.

Sincerely,
Jose

There are limits to a child's faith. In Juvie, I try to always honor those limits.

23

Another Reason

Most people ask how I can do what I do for a living. How can I deal with "those people" day in and day out? As if my families, rife with misfortune and misogyny, drugs and depravity, violence and voicelessness, exist in some other parallel world.

Even though we know that all families have at least a little something not so terrific to deal with, we still do not compare ourselves to the extreme examples that I have worked with in Juvie court.

So, why do I do it?

Here are some reasons why.

I was sitting on assignment when I recognized one of my former kids, Shonda. Shonda was in the back of the courtroom as I was hearing the case regarding the latest of her mother's children. She was a young lady now, working and in her own home. She was there as a prospective legal guardian to the child at issue. We visited off the record for a while, reminiscing, with the mother not the least bit apologetic or even interested in her child up for custody. How did this happen? How did this one child make it and grow up into a lovely, responsible woman? We gave all this mother's children the same chances, and gave the mother many years of services but to no avail. But Shonda, this one rose bloomed, and came back to rescue her little sister. Unless you do this kind of work for a living, you cannot begin to know the joy, exhilaration, and satisfaction I felt that day.

A big sister was saving her little sister from the system.

On another day, I was sitting again for a colleague who was out sick. I called the next case, and as I waited for the parties to enter the courtroom, a frisson of something started to buzz. The woman came in with a baby carrier, and I looked at her and smiled. Before I got a chance to say anything, she yelled, "It's you! I thought you were retired. I'm so happy to see you." I agreed, as I recognized one of my not so successful girls. Laura as a minor was quite the handful, willful and angry. Now here she was, a non-minor dependent, over the age of eighteen. There is a Californian law that allows for a young man or woman, upon reaching the age of eighteen, to apply to stay in the system under certain conditions. Our own children in foster care are expected to be tossed out with nothing at age eighteen, unless he or she is working at least twenty hours a week or in school. We will support foster youth to age twenty-one only if that child is working, preparing for a career, or continuing a college education. We supply a monthly check directly to the man or woman with regular hearings to make sure that that young person is on track.

Laura was one of those women who opted to stay in extended foster care until she turned twenty-one. She was nineteen in that courtroom that day, with a two-year-old and an adorable infant with her in court. We talked for a while, I played with her baby, then we got down to business. She was in school full time. She was training to be a social worker and work with foster children; her backup plan was nursing. She wanted to help others for a living. We beamed at each other, all past forgotten, me marveling at the miracle in front of me. She had done well, and I was there to see it. It was a very good day.

On that same day, I had an adoption on the calendar. One of our foster children, a little boy, aged two, was being adopted by the foster parents who so wanted a child. They were beside themselves with happiness. There are so many things that could happen between placement and permanency in Juvie. Not this time. The child was lively and loud. The adoptive parents got worried. Maybe this adoption wouldn't go through if he appeared to actually act like a child. I reassured them, we got Alex some paper and pens, and off we went with the proceeding. The whole finalizing of the adoption process takes about ten minutes, but it makes a family for life. They cried and kissed and came up to the bench for photos. Then off they left the courtroom to celebrate this enormously wonderful life-changing experience. They had cake. I was filled with the warm feeling that comes from being a part of one of the best days ever.

And these are the reasons why I worked in Juvie.

24

Behind That Decision to
Remove or Return a Child

As a juvenile court bench officer, we have much more discretion than other disciplines have. While we have statutes and case law precedent to guide us, as do all trial courts, we have a broad range of interpretations to anchor our decisions. Because we see so many different ages and ethnicities of people, even the same or similar fact patterns can lead to diametrically opposed findings.

We may have a petition of physical abuse against a parent. I look at the age of parent, instrument of abuse, background of family, rationale by parent for abuse. Then I used my instincts and my experience, and, because the law allows me to use inferences, I'd either return the children or remove them.

But sometimes what I should do, and what I want to do, are at war. In those moments, I strain to find a basis to do what I want. If I can't, I do what I must. With a heavy heart.

Take the young couple who came before me on an allegation of molest. They have a new baby boy. They had taken pictures of the husband and baby, which included his kissing the child's penis. They took the pictures to be developed (a situation which would not exist today) and the developer had contacted the police. They were arrested and the baby was removed. I took one look at these pictures and came to my own conclusion.

"How stupid and petty could people be to think this was abuse?" I said to myself.

But this couple had been arrested, and I could not return their baby. That baby had to stay out of their home until the criminal charges had been disposed of, and they were free to take the classes to prove they were not child abusers. I was so outraged by the treatment they received from the criminal justice system, while major molesters were out there, that I thought of contacting someone from the district attorney's office! But not even in my dreams could I do that. I was not their advocate, but the trier of fact, and held to the legal standards incumbent upon me. The couple eventually got their baby back, after an excruciating several months.

There was nothing I could do about what those poor parents had to go through.

Then there were those times when I knew what was better for the child, but it was against all the current law. And sometimes I was right, and sometimes I was wrong!

The most crucial times of decision are removal and return. There are specific standards for both. The standard in Juvie is not the unfitness of the parent, but the detriment to the child. Detriment to return, and detriment not to return. So sometimes I find there is no legal detriment, but in my heart, I know this will not work. This family is faking it. The batterer is just waiting for me to exit before returning home. The kids are still at risk of a substance-abusing parent, because dry is not sober. But because classes are done, plans are followed, the kids go back to a home that's not ready to have them. Then the kids come back, within six months usually, as what we knew in our hearts was exactly had happened. And the cycle begins again. Only this time, I have precedent to say that second time around I get to have a more stringent look at risk.

Then there is the relative versus the foster parent dilemma. The law requires that relatives, very broadly defined, have precedence for placement of children. There are several criteria in the law for what that means in terms of home study, morality, safety issues, and more.

But most prior criminal activity can be waived regarding relatives, and households can be minimal. What to do if all of grandma's kids are in jail? How many of her kids' kids can she handle in her little house? I can paint with a broad brush in either direction, but keep in mind that studies show kids do better with relatives, however marginal, than they do in foster care. And that grandma may have learned a thing or two since she got sober. So even though that foster home has a swimming pool, and no felony convictions to speak of, grandma wins. And mostly, that is a good thing.

Sometimes, however, it can cause severe heartache. To us all.

There was a couple who were very young. They were in my courtroom holding hands. They asked me to let them keep the baby girl who had been placed with them two months before. This baby was number eight for the birth mother, and because the child was born under the influence, she was immediately removed. There was no identified father, and the mother had not regained custody of any of her other children. The social worker placed the baby girl in a pre-adoptive home, apparently confident there would be no problem. This young couple had done the classes, and hoped, and prayed, and now they had their baby girl. They only had to wait for the legal system to work, and the baby would be theirs. But, at the dispositional hearing, grandma showed up. The grandma had siblings of this child, but she did not know the mother had given birth again. She heard somehow, and was in court to request her granddaughter. Oh, my. I ordered a home study, and while she was not in the greatest of circumstances, there was no impediment to her having her grandchild. Plus, there were siblings in the home. I had no choice. The grandma had the preference. Upon hearing this, the foster parents were sobbing. They told the court how they decorated her room, and how this little baby girl would get all their attention. It was beyond excruciating. I wanted so much to let them keep this baby. But the law and research prefer family, if possible, so I had to let her go.

25

In Juvie, "Blended Families" Take on a Different Meaning

You think you've seen it all, but then you haven't. You'd think you've heard it all. You haven't. The ability of people to be so perverse, and live in a way that's unthinkable to most of us, is the currency of Juvie. The fallout of parents' behavior is always the kids. They didn't ask to be born, we always hear, so why should the shame or abuse land on them? They certainly didn't ask to be born into a dysfunctional world, full of angst and turmoil. All children really want, and need, is someone to love them and keep them safe. Food, warmth, hugs, books, laughter are all wonderful additions to the life of a child, but basic nutrition, a roof over the head, and freedom from fear will do if that's all that can be offered. The lives of parents of children involved in Juvie aren't quite so simple. Their needs are complicated, and their choices lead to drama. Much more drama.

Here's a case that comes to mind. Graziella was very pretty, sexy, and seductive. She came into court wearing as little as possible, with a flounce and a wiggle. Obvious catnip to men. Or at least two of them. Brothers. When one was in jail, she went with the other, and vice versa. She had children with both brothers, and at some point violence spilled over between the men. Add alcohol, and we have a map for disaster. The brothers came to court and each asked for their own children, each citing the mother's relationship with the other. They each claimed alcohol abuse by the other, domestic violence with the other, abuse of each other's children. And on and on. Graziella, the mother, sat there, smirking. The only thing that interested her was the attention being paid to her by each man. All the kids ended up in foster care. One brother regained custody of his kids, and that case ended. The other children did not go home. Four children, half siblings and cousins at the same time, separated permanently. You need ancestry.com to know who is who and where they came from. And Graziella, well, she just went on to yet another man. Sheesh.

In another petition, it said, in various places, Jim Jones Sr. and Jim Jones Jr. Reading the petition, I thought to myself, "Come on, Department, can't you read your own report?" Well, it turned out, mea culpa, social worker. It was not an error after all. Children one and two were fathered by Senior, and children three, four, and five by Junior. Everyone seemed to get along just fine, except for the drugs. Both Senior and Junior sold them, and used them. Kids were then removed. Everyone repented, and got sober, and Senior and Junior got other means of employment. I returned the kids to their respective fathers. It was hard to figure this one out without a pencil and paper. Five children, some belonging to the father, some to the grandfather, same last names. There was also someone who was the father and brother, I think?

Then there are the incest families that we see in Juvie. Sandy had four children by her father. Candy had three children by her father. Henry's father was also his grandfather. Susan's father was also her uncle. And on and on it goes.

Here's another doozy. Tony lived with two sisters. Both were developmentally delayed. He had six adult children by other women. He had two children with one sister, and four with the other. All six were developmentally delayed. The allegations were physical abuse and domestic violence. The children were never returned. Tony's adult children took permanent custody of their step siblings. The six children were half siblings and first cousins.

I can only imagine family reunions with Juvie families. You need a scorecard to identify the players. But whatever the relationships, they all still need the same things that we all need. It is just sometimes hard to figure out who will provide them.

26

Sometimes, Judges See Why Parents Are the Way They Are

One of the most important parental lessons one learns is to be your child's advocate. Not a best friend, but a nurturing, supportive person. The person a child turns to for love, protection, values, and standards. Apart from those unspeakable abusive parents, that percentage who need to be put away from society for life, and never allowed to speak to any child again, most parents at least try to do some halfway reasonable job. These parents usually say something along the lines of, "I did the best I could with what I had," and as hard as that was to hear, based on their own upbringings, they meant it.

And I believed them.

I sometimes gave out medals for good report cards with applause in the courtroom, and I never had a parent present who did not beam with pleasure. They did not, or would not, understand that the domestic violence in the house, or the drug use, hurt their day-to-day lives with their children. When confronted, the parents made excuses.

"But the kids were not in the house."

"They were not in the room."

As if whatever happened when the kids weren't there happened in a vacuum. Trying to make parents understand that there was no safe zone for their conduct was the first step to recovery, repair, and reunion. The best way for this to happen was for the good "come to

Jesus" moment to happen with extended family members taking the lead and working out a plan for the whole family to get involved.

The best way for this not to happen was to have warring families, or classic enablers. I have had fathers whose daughters were molested threaten to kill Mom's new boyfriend or husband, who was the molester. Understandable. I have had families of in-laws so angry at each other that it made the Hatfields and McCoys look like BFFs. I had to have two bailiffs standing by as the warring family members filed into my courtroom, after yelling and screaming in the hall. If one side of the family had been the reason for the removal, they had been ostracized by the rest of the family, or threatened. Nerves were shot, tension was high, and sometimes it got so bad, the children had to be removed from the second or third relative's home, and go into a confidential foster home.

But my favorite parents, the ones who made me want to scream, and sometimes did, were the enablers. These enablers tended to be the parents of the parents whose children could do no wrong, for they raised great kids, and therefore took absolutely no responsibility for how their own kids turned out. It must've been too painful, or the parents of the parents dealing with removal were too egotistical to take in what was happening. And they would feel both entitled and angry in all their dealings with me.

This is how the process of a petition works. A petition to file for a removal of a child begins when it is written up and there are supporting documents as to why a child should be removed. The petition outlines the steps the social worker took before the filing, during the child welfare check investigation, and up to the decision to file. In the petition, during the investigation phase, one requirement is to interview as many people as possible, both for facts underlying in the petition and for possible homes for the children. The object is to determine whether there is a reason to file, if there is family support, and these things need to be worked out here in the petition to disrupt the children as little as possible. And there it is. The reason for the government's ability to intrude on the life of the family.

There were so many examples of a grandparent enabling the bad behavior of a child that it was hard to keep track. This enabling complicates everything for everyone. Like the maternal grandmother who never saw drug use, and vehemently denied that use, even though the mother and father lived with her for a year. Or the paternal grandmother who blamed the mother for her son's battery of the mother of her grandchildren. I had grandparents who were extremely prominent in the community, who insisted that their daughter's boyfriend was the only reason their daughter used drugs. Or vice versa.

And there were people like Betty. She was a grandmother who flew in all the way from a Midwestern state for every single hearing. She always sat in the back of the courtroom and glared at me, when she wasn't loudly talking as the lawyers argued. She never tried to see her grandchildren who were in foster care. She used ethnic slurs on her child's partner, as if that was the only reason for the problem. Because of her position, her daughter never did any programs and her kid never went home.

These parents were on their children's sides, but in the worst possible way. They continued to give money to their children, for rent and food, all of which was used for drugs. They continued to provide housing when their children were back on the streets. They blamed the system, and me, for being harsh or not understanding their children. They felt they had to choose between their children and grandchildren, and they would almost always choose their children and continue to justify their parenting.

I ordered Alanon and Narconon, which are adjunct programs to Alcoholics and Narcotics Anonymous for families of users. They help the addicted parents take responsibility and not enable them. I also ordered therapy for these grandparents and monitored visitation, if appropriate. Mostly, my recommendations did not work. Sigh.

I would tell the parents of children facing removal that taking responsibility for their actions and understanding that actions have consequences are basic to healing, and will give them a new lease on life.

I have stated many a times in the courtroom, "If your parents continue to blame everyone else, it is easy for you to do the same."

It is kind of like this new thinking of everyone in the class getting an award, for everything. No winners or losers. No more best or worst. No more striving, because there are no reasons to soar. How sad, how debilitating, how unproductive. Standards, ethics, and values are all we pass on to our kids. Make them count.

27

Sometimes Judges Get Burnout

I spent a lot of time in Juvie saying, "But why?" Why would you do that? Why would you say that? Why would any normal person act that way? Well, they wouldn't. I've seen firsthand what poverty and desperation do to people's worldview. I have also seen paranoia, relentless egomania, stupidity, cupidity, and just plain meanness.

There are people in my world for whom two-year-olds are the major breadwinner in the family. Third-generation welfare families with no incentive to rise past that monthly check. Sadistic men who get their only gratification by abusing those weaker than they. Where drug use is rampant, insidious, and passed on. Where alcohol is considered a food staple. Men who cheat as a matter of course, and women who love them anyway. Women who sacrifice their children to keep a man in the home. Women with many children with different last names.

To people with those lives, we think, "If you know better, why don't you behave better?" Surely they know better.

But you know what I have learned? They don't know better. In their world, instant gratification is the only gratification there is. There is no long-term anything. Growing up, they did not have the luxury of learning values and ethics, consequences and accountability. So they live from day to day, from hour to hour, from minute to minute. They were raised that way, and so they raise their kids that way.

They are, for the most part, in a box, with the four walls of poverty, violence, fear, and lack of family support. For these parents, I am, or try to be, a door. I try to open the door with hope, with alternatives, with affirmatives. I'm the Queen of Rah-Rah, and yes, I reward, and praise. But then, oftentimes, I hit a wall.

Here is a random day as an example. I have thirty cases to hear. In all thirty cases, all the parents have done nothing on their plans. All the kids are failing their classes in school, if they are going at all. I have three teenagers who have run away, two who returned to their pimps. Then I get two new cases that have been filed in my court. They both are babies born under the influence, and these babies are children of parents who have been in my court before. One is baby number three; another is baby number eight.

Neither mother has regained custody of any of her other children. Rah-rah. Sigh. I feel myself getting frustrated, icily separating myself from my staff, the lawyers, and the families. I forget to talk to the children. I speed through the cases, without recapping or discussing moving forward. I am in self-protective mode because I feel myself taking the failure of these families personally. Sometimes I need to tell myself to breathe. I take a fifteen-minute break. Then I start again.

It often feels as if when Pandora opened that box, all the ills flew out and came directly to Juvie. But still, as in the myth, hope remains. So I hope. And I hope, as I know the kids hope that life will turn around for the better.

Emily Dickinson once said, "Hope is the thing with feathers that perches in the soul." It is the soul that seems to be the throwaway in a life that has minute-to-minute concrete needs. It is the soul we need to find, to tap into the deepest understanding that you are entitled to all that life has to offer. That your soul is the same as others, and needs nurturing by adding values and ethical behavior to your daily choices. We go to the baby steps, and try to do the "three good things to one bad thing" maxim. Rah, one clean test. Rah, parenting classes going well. Rah, good visits with the kids. Great, but wait, no counseling sessions, and still no housing? Working? To the kids, are you in school?

Being in the position I am in, I cannot help but wonder, "Why oh why am I doing this?" In between depression and anger, I'm starting to believe I have Stockholm Syndrome, where a person who is kept against her will decides to ally herself with the captor. Days when I felt that way are not good days. I end those long days of hopelessness still hoping tomorrow will be better.

28

Sexually Abused Children

Today we talk about the closest crime to murder one can due to a child. Molestation, especially from one who is supposed to be the protector of life and body, kills the soul of a child. There are as many forms of molest as there are perpetrator and participants. But if you do this work for a living, we can divide up the behaviors into accessible categories.

I once dated a man who did not like a particular friend of mine. He did not like my friend because she called me every day with a litany of woes, all real, and all consuming. I listened, advised, sympathized, and offered what assistance I could, as her friend. The man I was seeing said I was looking more and more dejected after each phone call. He said to me, "You know, your body doesn't know whose crap it is listening to." In other words, unhappiness taken in day after day affects your mind and spirit, even if is not your own unhappiness.

Those words have resonated with me when I parsed out the level of abuse in the cases I worked with. Is this a small child or a teenager? A natural child or a stepchild? Was there violence? Threats? Pregnancy? Did the other parent know? As I watched the victim testify, or the perpetrator explain, I wondered what I have given up in my soul to listen to these accounts. I was always aware that I had limited time and access to these children, but in those moments, it took everything within me to make the most of those times, to do what I could to make those children whole again.

A violation of boundaries and unwanted touch to the body are beyond reprehensible, but rape and molest are not the same. Although they may cross over, they do not have the same penalties at law or in dependency. Rape is mostly not about sex, but domination and power in the mind of a rapist. If there is a rape alleged, I frequently see the alleged perpetrator in court in jail blues. With molest, I am frequently looking at the alleged perpetrator in front of me, not arrested. I also find a disturbing number of women supporting the molester against her children. There are some mothers who are in competition with their much younger daughters, and will do, say, or believe anything to keep the man at home. Some women trade their girls, or boys, for the stability of an income provided by the molester. To tell the truth on what is happening is to put the whole family in jeopardy, especially if this is a family cycle where the mother or father were abused.

To the rapist and molesters, the line between adult and child is blurred. The cry, "She seduced me," is frequently proffered. Did the fifteen-year-old girl have sex with her forty-year-old stepfather for the promise of a car at sixteen? Possibly. But how do you get across to that man that he is in charge of that transaction, and bound to neither offer nor accept.

Frequently we see "grooming," a term used to describe a slow seduction of a child. Small hugs and caresses lead to longer and more intimate behavior until the child is fully engaged. If this happens with a loved parent, and feels good, it often takes years before any reports happen. The man or woman excuses this behavior by calling it "love" or preparation for adult sex with a spouse. It is despicable, and can damage children for a lifetime. It would have to take years with specific therapy for the children to not self-blame and to heal all that was done to them.

When I was an attorney, I once represented a man who had met his fourteen-year-old daughter for the first time, after an acrimonious split from her mother. She sought him out, and when she found him, they fell in love. It did no good to continue to tell him that what he was doing was wrong, for he didn't want to hear it. His current wife said he could not be a pedophile because he was not a homosexual. This is the level of stupidity we had to deal with! Halfway through that particular case, with a restraining order in place, and ongoing specialized therapy, the father and daughter disappeared, and we never saw them again. Molestation? Of course.

These children and youth experience grooming through seduction by financial promises, or preferential treatment, to threats and violence from the other parent who looks the other way. The only way they can avoid being violated is when a parent actually stands up, like this one woman, one of my favorite mothers, who, upon finding out her daughter was being molested by her boyfriend, popped him hard with an iron skillet. She ended up being in jail while he recovered in the hospital. I wished her well.

I am happy to say that I did see my fair share of parents who reacted appropriately, swiftly, and decisively when they heard their children were being abused. Women who immediately left their men, called the police, reported the molest, and supported their children through the systems. I saluted them, and did what I could to help them start a new life, often without the primary breadwinner.

When in the midst of these stories, I contemplated what I had given up to hear these cases and wondered if I had lost the ability to be shocked. At first, when you bear witness to these stories of childhood sexual abuse, you are shocked beyond belief. But after hearing hundreds of cases of similar stories with the same old patterns and circumstances playing out, a part of you reacts differently to these cases. You are not shocked anymore. Maybe it's self-protection because it won't help the child to become emotional, even though your heart goes out to them. It made my heart sing when I could celebrate the resilience and courage of the victims and their strong families. I always tried to make sure the child victims, both by the molester and unprotective parent, were placed in a loving home forever, with either a relative who gets it, or, more often, with an older sibling who has survived.

29

Abandoned Children

You have had your first, second, third baby. Or more. You are exhausted, tired, spent, and you haven't been dressed in a week. It is the middle of summer, and you have no air-conditioning. The kids have either been crying all day, or two of them have heat rashes. Your husband or partner gratefully escapes as soon as possible each morning.

Can you relate?

Parents have all been there, overextended and overwhelmed. We've all wanted out. Just for a day. Just for an hour. Please, please give me a hot shower, and silence. Maybe a cup of tea. Maybe something a bit stronger.

If you are one of those people lucky enough to be organized and calm, with a supportive and hands-on partner, well, good for you. The rest of us envy you in a way you can't imagine. But suppose you are living a normal life. The kids are pretty normal, some may be in school all day, and work is not a problem. Money is tight, but enough to meet the family needs. If there is enough support is in place, what then would make a mother leave her children? And what would make her come back?

One of the nastiest parts of Juvie is having a parent who has no perceivable reason for the actions which bring the children into court. As a bench officer, my job is to help the children and the family, repair the damage that threatens them. But what if there is no damage? What if a mother abandons her kids because of vanity, or indifference, or narcissism, or self-involvement. Those cases always filled me with disgust. Anger. Frustration. But I could not show how I felt in front of the children. I often failed though. It just made my blood boil. My face would get red. My voice strained. I would ask these mothers over and over again whether they were planning on getting housing, rehab, therapy? The answer was often no, or a shrug. She would then leave the way she came, and we never saw her again.

I was used to those kinds of behaviors from fathers, and would be almost surprised whenever one stepped up. I know that is biased, but the sheer number of cases created that presumption. In my decades of courtroom experience, fathers usually were not the primary caretakers. So, whenever a mother deliberately abandoned her children, it really caused some deep emotions.

I understand that some mothers are so deep in their addictions that any attempt at parenting is out of the question. Also, some mothers are mentally ill to such a degree that they cannot meet each child's daily needs. Those cases I get, but what about those others?

There was one mom who actually showed up in court when she got a notice. She had taken her four children to the child welfare county department offices, and told the staff there that they should find homes for them. When I saw this mother in court, I looked at her intently.

"Why did you do that? What were you thinking?"

This mother shrugged and told me matter-of-factly, "Look, my boyfriend isn't interested in paying for some other man's kids. So they have to go."

This mother said this right in front of her kids, who were all standing there in court. I made a motion and out the mother went. She never made an attempt to be with her kids again.

Another mother, this one had five children by two different men. She had two children with Dad 1 and three with Dad 2. She was living with Dad 2 and came to court over allegations that Dad 2 physically abused her two children, the ones she had with Dad 1. All the children were removed. Luckily, Dad 1, the father of the older two children, was able to take them, and while he had not been hands on before, he showed himself willing to be. These older children didn't want to be separated from their siblings though. They desperately wanted to return to their mother's home. But she didn't want them, and she refused to do any counseling with them, or even visit. Since there were no allegations regarding the natural children of Dad 2, those three younger children were eventually returned. The two eldest children ended up with a custody order with their biological dad; no contact with their stepfather, Dad 2; and monitored visits with their mother. She had not seen them once throughout the case history. She just abandoned them.

Then there was the mother who had a lengthy history of drug addiction. She had disappeared many years before, and her boys had grown up in the foster care system. They were luckily always together in the same home. They were a challenge. Always on the brink of some disaster or other, but had remained out of the juvenile justice system so far. They were both nearing eighteen, and were actually somewhat stable. School was good, future plans were being made, and they were finally moving ahead with confidence. Then, at one hearing, the mother showed up out of the blue after years of not being in her kids' lives. There she was, in the back of the court, telling me she wanted her kids back. They were elated. I was not. I asked her to contact the Department, to check out her home, her circumstances, her ability to even see her kids in a non-supervised setting. She was incensed that I would even question her.

She then said, "Thank you for taking care of my children, I would like them back now, if you please."

I didn't please. Her lack of self-awareness and entitlement was astounding. We had a tense moment. The boys were furious with me. I moved past their anger and set for the next hearing to be in about a month, to get some answers.

Two weeks later, there was a special hearing. Both boys had run away, and were living with their mother. The older boy had been arrested, as the mother and her new boyfriend, about whom we knew nothing, had recruited the boys as drug couriers. The older boy, Lance, had been caught. His mother had not appeared in delinquency court. Abandoned again. I tried to talk the younger boy, Fred, into going back to this original foster home, but was unsuccessful. I would place him in another foster home. He would run. We would issue a warrant, and go out and get him at his mother's home. School was over. Plans were over. And soon, Fred had been arrested also. Both boys ended up in the juvenile justice system, because of a mother whose only aim was her own self-preservation.

I have trouble with children being seen and treated as widgets. I have trouble with our United States government thinking of children as widgets, so to contemplate a child's mother thinking of them that way, it kills something in me and makes me, on some level, deep down, a bit homicidal.

I try to tell my courtroom kids that they may see their abandoning parents as soon as they start making money. I tell them to not be seduced when that day comes, but largely it is to no avail. The kids usually take the parents back with open arms as the siren song of family and belonging is too strong. We all want to know who we come from, and if we are lucky, where we belong. And these kids will do almost anything to make that happen.

Sometimes the love of the parent to the child is not as strong as the love of a child to a parent. I do what I can in those cases and hope that someday, the child will see their parents for who they really are, and not internalize that they are the reason for their abandonment.

30

Four Dads

There are four dads you should know about. I have so many stories about dads, but these dads resonated with me. I want to show the best and worst of them.

Manuel had three daughters and one son. He sold Chrissy, his twelve-year-old daughter, to a friend of his. When they left the house, Chrissy's grandfather, Jose, called the police. Thankfully, the friend and Chrissy were stopped at the border.

The friend was arrested, and the petition was filed. Chrissy's grandfather said that his son had a van with a mattress in the back. He would park it in the neighborhood to operate his business with his girls. Manuel's only son, aged thirteen, was rented to a thirty-year-old woman regularly. The other two girls were teenagers, fourteen and fifteen.

Manuel was never arrested, and promised me he would do nothing I asked him to do. He also promised me that his children would never stay in foster care, as they would run away back to him, no matter what I did. I sent the kids to therapy, but they never went, and they never made a week in foster care. This filthy, completely nasty man had them brainwashed to such a degree that they, and their sad, faded mother, believed they could not exist without him. It was terrifying and frustrating in equal parts.

He was right, and finally he and the children realized that we would continue to find them and remove them from the home, so he had them moved. We never found out where they lived.

When I faced Manuel, I told him I would keep the case open until all his children turned eighteen, and I did. The only time we saw any of his kids again was when the twelve-year-old, who then was sixteen, had a baby, which also led to petition of removal. When the baby was born, the hospital was not comfortable with the information given by the mother regarding her competence. When Chrissy came to court, Manuel tried to say that he was the father, and Chrissy's mother was the mother, as that was the name she put on the birth certificate. I knew, of course, that Chrissy's mother wasn't the baby's mother, but I did a paternity test to make sure Manuel wasn't the father. If he was the father, I could have him arrested and prisoners don't take too kindly to pedophiles. It turned out that my instincts were right. Manuel, thankfully, wasn't the father.

I put Chrissy's baby in foster care, ordered no contact by Manuel or the baby's grandmother. Chrissy disappeared after the hearing and the baby was adopted by the foster parents.

John had two daughters, Gwen and a newborn, Mary. John lived with Mary's mother, and regularly saw Gwen's mother. One day, when that child was visiting, John and Mary's mom had an altercation which led to a neighbor calling the police. A petition was filed. Everyone was there: Gwen's mother, Mary's mother, and John. I released Gwen back to her mother's custody, as she was not involved in the confrontation. John left the home he shared with Mary's mother, and with his lawyer's promises that he would stay away from the family home. Because of this, I released Mary to her mother. John was very remorseful and assured me with earnest and smiling enthusiasm that he would do all I asked to return home. In my mind I dubbed John "Charming Dad." I set the next hearing date at six months. Both moms had custody of their children, and because Mary's mom was to have no contact with John, Mary and her child left the building. John decided to go to the cafeteria for lunch, and while in line, he met a young woman who was also in court for her children. She had drug issues. They apparently hit it off. So much nicer to share lunch, *n'est-ce pas**? Did I mention he was charming?

At the next hearing, two things happened. John and Mary's mother were in complete compliance and I had already increased his visits to unmonitored. I asked Mary's mom if she was ready to have John home, and she indicated they had done some serious soul-searching and she was. Why the soul searching? Because there was a new petition filed that involved John. He had a preemie born under the influence with the young woman he met at lunch. John looked rueful. I had to laugh. Many serious batterers present as charming to outsiders, but this guy was not a batterer. He had made a mistake and did the work to fix it. I set a six-month review.

At the review hearing, the young lunch lady was still using, and rarely seeing her latest baby, which was her pattern with the other children she had lost. John and Mary's mom wanted that baby to raise with her half-sibling. I couldn't believe Mary's mom would take another woman's child, but she had no hesitation. I returned the prematurely born child to John's full custody, and told him to stay out of the cafeteria. After that, I got a nice Christmas card, and I never saw this family again.

That's a win in my business.

Burt had one child, the youngest of Sally's four children. Sally had a history of drugs and mental health issues. Burt was the only father we found and he was noticed to come to court.

From the top of his shaved head to all I could see of his neck, arms, hands, he was tattooed. This was a scary-looking dad. You would cross the street if he came toward you at night. Burt also had an arrest history. When he asked to have his child released to him, I told him it was too early in the process. He was visibly angry at my ruling. After the next hearing, all of Sally's children were placed in foster care. There were no relatives who came forward. Burt, however, did and asked to address the court.

"Could I visit with all the children, not just mine?" Burt asked.

I was surprised by this request, but granted it upon the children's response. The children said it was okay for him to visit them and so he did.

At the six-month review, Burt was clean, sober, working, and more even tempered. Sally was completely gone and had done nothing on her plan to regain custody, not even a visit. All the children were present in court this time around, as children over four came to court in LA. Burt was festooned with them. His child was on his lap, while the others clutched to whatever part of him they could reach. Burt then asked me a question.

"Referee Sobel, I'd like to have custody of all four children."

There was not a dry eye in that place, including mine. I exited out of the case with Burt having full custody of his child and legal guardianship of the older three. All the children and Burt smiled and hugged each other.

What's that old adage about a book and its cover?

Jose was a lifer. He was at Pelican Bay, California's toughest prison. Jose was sentenced for life without parole. Jose insisted on being in court for the first hearing regarding his young teenage boy, Jose Jr., who was removed because of his mother's drug use. Jose was brought in on a bus and housed in one of our internal jail cells. At the hearing, where Jose and his son were very emotional, Jose asked through his attorney not to come back to court again.

I was going to say something but, with tears in his eyes, Jose then spoke for himself.

"I can't come back. I can't handle what a mess I made of my life, your honor...I don't want my son to see me like this."

His son was crying, he clearly wanted to see his dad.

Even though Jose was doing hard time, I could tell that he loved his son. I tried to offer some hope.

"Jose. It is not too late to make a good lasting impact on your son. You could be the best role model ever. You are a perfect example of what not to do in life. Write your son letters every day. Parent in those letters. Help him find good values, and make better choices."

Jose's eyes seemed to dry up when I gave this advice. I continued to tell him that he did not have to be present to be a guide for his child's life.

Near the end of the hearing, Jose nodded and promised that he would follow through on my advice.

"Your honor, may I hug my son before I go?"

I said yes, and his son ran up to his father, who was in cuffs. They had a long, tearful goodbye.

According to Jose's son, who did very well in his placement, his father wrote every day, and he cherished those letters.

31

My Professional Photo Is Not Professional

I have been very lucky in ending up with a thirty-year-and-counting career that satisfies me in every way. I've also been lucky enough to have people in charge who allowed me free rein to fulfill all my nutty dreams. And finally, I was lucky enough to have some of those dreams come true, and change the way things were done in child welfare. As a result of my years of work, supportive work from colleagues, and luck, I have frequently been asked to speak at national venues, or I've been honored by various community groups. It's been an amazing ride.

As each group prepared whatever program I was involved with, I was always asked for a photograph. I sent the same one every time. I occasionally got some pushback, but I asked they use that photo. In programs, and once in a huge poster, my chosen picture was used each time.

So, what the heck is the problem?

Well, I promised my grandson to take him to the National Finals of the Monster Truck Rally in Las Vegas, at the University of Nevada Las Vegas arena. So, off we went: me, my grandson, his parents, his best friend, and his best friend's mother. I rented a suite so we could be together, and we arranged ourselves in the beautiful rooms, and got ready for the weekend. My daughter and her friend set up spa days and shows, while Norm and I took my grandson and his best friend to the arena for the monster truck rally.

It took forever to get into the arena as it was fully sold out with thousands and thousands of people attending. I bought everyone

Monster Truck shirts, flags, and foam fingers, and in we went, past dozens of booths filled with tons of American junk food. I mean junk food. Yum. I have spent over thirty years dealing with families in crisis. With negligence and the worst parenting. But there I was, on another planet. Thousands of families were there to cheer on their favorite monster trucks, in one of the most bizarre weekends in which I have ever participated. You had to wear earphones as the noise was deafening. Between the trucks and the audience, rabid fans all, you couldn't hear anyone. The trucks were huge, elaborately decorated, and so were the drivers. They ran heats and races through an elaborate makeshift course. The woman who was sitting in front of me had her favorite truck tattooed on her neck, and her two kids on her lap.

Eventually, we made eye contact.

"Isn't this fun," I had managed to yell out so she could hear me. She turned, smiled, and gave me a thumbs up. "Oh, hell yeah!"

The arena was filled with people having fun. Fun! Nothing like what I would ever have expected. At some point, I was up screaming for Gravedigger, when Norm snapped a picture of me. I didn't see it coming but it captured a great moment. It was not very professional, but it's my favorite. Why? Because it reminds me there are families in this country who are doing the best they can to be good parents and live an authentic life. Because it reminds me to never take myself seriously, no matter what. And that no one else should confuse my message, no matter how serious, with my personality. That I am accessible, and welcome input. I have had so much fun, doing what I love.

And I have the photo to prove it.

32

Six Months of Being More Than a Judge

There is a regular debate within the child welfare system as to the function of a juvenile court judge. What is our role? What is our reach? In regular civil or criminal cases, the role of the participants is crystal clear. Trial protocol is followed, juries are empaneled, the judge presides. Juvie is different, a Wild West in comparison. Our mandate is to reach into the community to help solve our families' problems. Many of our judges don't agree with that, and stick very strictly to the idea of judicial restraint. They interpret the law and make decisions based on case law, and statutes. Others gleefully give regularly unasked for, and probably unappreciated, advice and nose into all parts of the lives of our families.

I am one of the latter. I don't believe my job ends with the workday either. My work continues in committees, in teaching other new bench officers, attending and presenting at seminars, and making whatever difference I can from day to day.

Being a Juvie Bench Officer is more than a day job. It's a calling.

There was a six-month-period in my time on the bench that probably would have been considered extremely inappropriate by my more conservative judicial friends and colleagues. To me, it was the essence of who I am, and why I do this work. Allow me to share an example of what my fellow more conservative judges would never do.

The six-month period started out with an invitation from Michelle, one of my teenaged girls. She was allowed to invite three adults to attend her high school graduation. She was in a group home, and had worked like an Amazonian warrior to gain her stability and prosper. And she did. Michelle's dad and mom were out of the picture. The invitations were sent to me, her social worker, and her attorney. Would I go? You bet! All three of us took balloons and yelled our heads off when Michelle got her diploma. She had to have heard us! We were so proud. Then I found out that she had won a scholarship to a very prestigious culinary institute. It was a great night. We took her out to celebrate. After that wonderful evening, Michelle stopped in once to see me at court, before she faded into her own life.

A few weeks later, I opened my newspaper to read about a disastrous car chase. When the police chased the car, the driver ended up smashing into a wall. His passenger, named Sade, was a seventeen-year-old foster child. She was killed. She was one of mine. She shouldn't have been in that car. But Sade was obstreperous, difficult, a frequent runaway, a school dropout, then drop in. The fact that she broke the rules was not a surprise. But even though we warned and warned about how dangerous it was "out there," we didn't expect our kids to die because of it.

Shortly after I got the news, her attorney paid a visit to my chambers. "Sherri, are you going to the funeral?"

I was almost insulted that she asked. "Yes, I'll be there."

I had had children die during my time on the bench, but not like this. At the funeral, I said a few words, then let the congregation of her foster mother, who was paying for the funeral, take over. Sade's father was at the funeral and spoke. Her mother came from Texas to see if any money was forthcoming from the police car chase. When she was told no, she went home and did not attend the church ceremony. The church was filled with the foster mother's congregation. It was warm and loving.

Rest in peace, Sade.

A few months after the funeral, I had a hearing with Jerry, one of my young men. Like many of them, he was quiet and hard to reach.

He lacked any ambition I could detect, and I couldn't get a handle on how to help him. Then, somehow, he discovered wrestling, and he was home. He excelled and he knew he had to keep his grades up to stay on the team. And he did. In one court hearing, he told me that he was representing his team in a state wrestling championship tournament. It was happening in a city not far from my home.

This got my attention. "Jerry, would it be okay if I came and watched?"

Jerry smiled. "Yeah! That would be awesome. The tournament is at..."

My husband and I went on the day of the matches and found pandemonium! There were four or five matches going on all over the gym, with whistles blowing, people yelling, and young kids running all around. I thought it would be impossible to find Jerry, let alone watch his match. When we entered the bleachers, a man came over to us.

"Are you the judge here for Jerry?"

I told him I was his Referee just as I saw Jerry across the way in his wrestler's outfit. I waved and he ran right over.

"Thank you for coming!" Jerry said.

"I wouldn't miss it, are you kidding me?" I said back.

Jerry then invited my husband and me to sit right on the gym floor where he was to wrestle. I was touched and proud, and very excited when he decisively defeated all opponents to take the state prize in his group. After the tournament, Jerry ran up to me with the biggest smile on his face.

"You did it! I'm so proud of you!" I said as we hugged a sweaty hug.

We chatted a bit more before he ran off with his friends.

What a day!

The six-month period of visiting kids outside the courtroom ended with Javon. He was a beautiful baby, but he was very damaged, developmentally delayed and riddled with disease. His mother had abandoned him, and he had been placed, several months prior, in the home of foster parents who cared for him day in and day out. Then we all found out he had very little time left due to his ailments. The foster parents wanted to adopt him, but the mother showed up in court and decided that there might be some money attached to his condition, which was the only reason why she wanted him back. The termination of parental rights and the possibility of appeal took months. Months Javon shouldn't have had. But he made it. Barely. I set the adoption hearing for the foster parents just days before he died. I went to the funeral and spoke of the dedication and love that kept Javon on this earth long enough to forever belong to the people who were rightfully his parents.

Case law? Just making judicial decisions? Not in this lifetime.

33

Hallelujah! Amen!

Day after day, we bring in the parents who are in custody. They come in on special busses, from local jails or state prisons. We make arrangements for appearances by telephone for Federal prisoners, or any prisoner not permitted by law to attend court. We cross every T. We dot every I so that we protect these parents' constitutional right to be present at the hearings regarding their children. It may also be the only time a visit happens for the kids and parent.

The thing is, many of these people—and I already know what you are going to say, but don't bother, I've heard it before—are poverty prisoners. The same behavior from a rich college student would get little time, if any, and community service. I am not excusing the bad behavior, just putting it in perspective. Low-level drug use, or sales, minor theft, we seem to get a lot of prisoners with basic time to serve. Which will mean less time to find a job, less ability to find a job, less time with the family, and now with a criminal record. Sorry, I digress.

We also get prisoners brought in who are major in the crime world. Murderers, doing life, credit card rackets, and identity theft on a worldwide basis. Serial rapists, and violent men and women who pose a risk to society forever, no matter how much time they actually spend in jail or prison. But they come to court, for the most part, respectful to me, and grateful for any time they get with their children.

We get an occasional angry, disrespectful, rude, "who cares" parent. I make sure the hearing is quick and pared down with those folks. Bye.

This one day that I recall was no different. Dad was in custody. Mom came in carrying the youngest of her four children. In the back of the courtroom was the paternal grandmother and two paternal aunts. Everyone waved and blew kisses at the dad. It was really surreal to see that it did not appear to be shameful to stand in front of your family and children in jail blues. You wonder what kind of values are acceptable, or what standards are accepted to not be upset with family members in custody. I really couldn't understand it. And I was not really delighted to see them there celebrating this person.

Many thoughts crossed my mind when I saw Mom coo to her little baby boy, nearly a year old, about Dad.

"There's your Daddy. Wave to Daddy. Hi, Daddy!"

For some reason, that day, I had had it! I turned to the father.

"You. Look at your child. Do you love your son?"

He smiled, "Of course I do. I love all my children."

It took every ounce of self-control not to scream, but I did raise my voice.

"Then you need to get out of jail, and live a decent life, and stop waving at your children from a jail cell!"

I took a breath and suddenly remembered that his mother and sisters were in the back of the courtroom. Oops! I was hoping I would not get taken too much over the coals when, suddenly, the dad's mother shouted from the back.

"Hallelujah!"

Right after that, the sisters shouted out, "Amen!"

We all started to laugh. It was needed.

I was still chuckling a little as I said, "I didn't realize we were having a revival meeting, but if it helps the father change his life, then I'm all for it."

The dad had the good grace to laugh. He then made me a promise.

"Your honor, you will never see me in jail blues again."

I believed him and he proved me right. I never saw him in my courtroom again.

108

34

Nine Kids in One Family

It was one of those days. Mom and Dad had eight kids. Mom came in for the hearing carrying baby number nine. Other than the first child, the dad was the same for all the rest. That is very unusual.

We were at a six-month review hearing. The parents had done nothing to get their children back. Absolutely nothing. Mom had spent the hearing breastfeeding her ninth baby. The parents only asked for bus passes and money for services. I couldn't help but notice Dad's green and specially barbered hair, and Mom's beautiful jewelry.

I looked at the report, which was essentially a book. I was scanning the medical, educational, and psychological status of each child plus updates and status on parents' participation, if any. An explanation needed to be included as to why the services were not done, according to the parents.

Child No. 1 was psychotic and violent. Fifteen-years-old. In a group home, but needing a more restrictive placement. Probably a locked hospital ward, which is problematic in California. School was a no. Meds were not being taken.

Child No. 2, thirteen-years-old, had been seen running around the neighborhood screaming at unknown people. Education was a no. Meds were taken. Foster home requested removal.

Child No. 3, twelve-years-old, was in a specialized group home for children with mental health issues. School was okay, meds were being taken.

Child No. 4, eleven-years-old, was in a group home. Mental health issues, but attending school. Meds.

Child No. 5, ten-years-old, was in foster care. Mental health issues, school okay, meds.

Child No. 6, eight-years-old, was in foster care. School okay, some developmental disabilities, no meds.

Child No. 7, five-years-old, was in foster care. School okay, some developmental disabilities, on meds. Mild treatment for ADHD.

Child No. 8, two-years-old, had developmental disabilities. Was receiving community assistance by our Regional Center, which was the deliverer of services to our disabled children.

And then child No. 9. I wondered why this child had not been removed yet. We had the hearing, and I, with a loud sigh, continued these parents' services.

How on earth could we help this family? Ongoing drug use, mental health issues, developmental problems, nine children, no money, no jobs, no nothing. Right after the hearing, I received a warrant asking me to sign to remove baby No. 9. I signed and sighed again.

Just shoot me.

35

The Spiral Syndrome

If you have not, in the dead of night, thought to yourself, "Tie someone's tubes, male or female, please!" then you have not dealt with dependency.

One of the most interesting and frustrating dynamics during my thirty years, both as an attorney and as a bench officer, has been what I call "the spiral syndrome." That phrase refers to the ongoing generational abuse in families. I have represented children, parents, grandparents, each in the system, first as abused, then as an abuser.

As the years have gone by, I have pondered and worried over what we must be doing wrong the first time around. How did we fail these families from our end?

I was what you call an "activist referee." I would interact with the families, talk regularly with them, yell, promise, use the carrot, use the stick. Anything to get children to a safe, permanent home. I have been told by some relatives that I scare parents straight, or by a few parents that I was the first person to really listen to them, and offer help.

Yet, no matter what I did, what services were offered, back they came. Over and over. A child, two, or more. Like this one mother, Alisha, who got her kids back, and there would be an overwhelming sense of achievement and joy until, six months later, there's a new baby, and back she'd come and many more like her. Alisha had relapsed. The children wanted to go to Grandma, but Alisha had been removed from Grandma, years earlier, so we looked at Great-Grandma as a possibility. It turned out that Grandma was removed

111

from Great-Grandma even more years ago. How did I know this? Two reasons: One, it is in the Department's reports. But, more importantly, I knew them all! I had been the bench officer for all three generations!

Into my court they came, all of them. Each time they saw me, they broke into huge smiles because I knew these families, the siblings, the aunts and uncles. I asked about everyone and was shown pictures of new babies, not in the system, and other relatives.

There was another interesting aside to these cases. The older the adult, the less they can picture a woman on the bench. So Great-Grandma calls me "sweetie" or "honey" or even by my first name. The lawyers were always horrified, and apologetic. I laughed because it didn't bother me. It wasn't about the title; it was about the cure. I believed I was the conduit to safety for families, and I took failure personally. I didn't care how much they liked me and sometimes, I'd tell them, "Don't be so happy to see me!" and they'd nod and smile. My position was to get another crack at them, and that time we would break the cycle.

Always in those cases, I would explain, again, what they already know. Moms and dads need to get clean and sober, or domestic violence needs to be addressed. But none of my words will help without reasonable housing, good education, and job training. These were the cases we saw the most. These were the bread-and-butter cases, where we actually knew how to fix the families. But drug use was so insidious, and frustration levels so low, that it was almost impossible to eradicate in the time we had to work. Oftentimes, I found that by the time I had the third group in, Great-Grandma and Grandma were both sober, working, and really good role models for their grandchildren, if not for their children.

What kept me going was that, despite knowing that the definition of insanity was doing the same thing over and over and expecting a different result, miracles occasionally did happen. Also, families who still showed up and were trying, with no resources, no jobs, always no education, and many times, language barriers. With everything that I know, sometimes I think about what I would do if I were in charge of it all, and how some of it would infuriate the most liberal minded, and some of it would infuriate the conservatives.

I can say this, without a complete overhaul of the current system, our miracles will be far outdone by our failures, which will no doubt produce another generation of abused children. Now, if it were up to me, I would have a task force including medical, law enforcement, religious institutions, and schools work together identifying at-risk families. I would then use the Department of Children and Family Services to refer and assist with services to avoid filing a petition. I would do the same if a petition is filed, working within the community to get home faster, or get kids permanence faster. Child Welfare and Juvenile Justice are community problems requiring a community response. It saddens me that we as a system remain fragmented, arguing over turfs rather than coming together to help people.

36

Do Not Lump All Families Together

So, I hear you are all a little tired of bad news. I get it. I can't go anywhere without someone asking me about the latest injured or, worse, deceased child. Or ten kids living in unimaginable squalor or abuse.

Welfare generations, people without a dime for food yet have plenty of money for drugs. People who lack education and have no incentive to move up and out. People with little to no job skills, and no incentive to move up and out. On and on.

I get it.

Last week, as I was cleaning out a cabinet, I came across an envelope filled with notes, pictures, and letters. They all said somewhat the same thing. It worked. We are good. Thank you! I reread them all. Every one of them. Standing there, going through those letters, I thought that I had never seen any one of those families back in my court. Thinking about them more, I wondered why. Then something came to me that was so silly, I could hardly fathom it.

If you have become so rehabilitated that you took the time to write a personal note, you were really rehabilitated. Adding the niceties of life, a pause to say thanks, a more appropriate outfit in court tells me, and tells you, that "up and out" has occurred.

Sure, we get families back, from grandma to mom to daughter to grandchild, year after year, and they take the classes, again, and do the services, again, and then leave. No stable housing, no job, no support, so no real strides. Then we have families where the services are step one. Where getting a job or training is step two. And where the kids are regularly in school, with visits by the parents stressing reading and homework.

Do not lump all my families together. Life is hard at the bottom of the barrel, and swimming up is against the constraints of background, language, and beliefs. We know color is an issue, we know race is an issue, but you all tend to ignore the upper-class families we get. So, we concentrate on the not so simple plan of re-raising an entire family, and how do we measure success? In two ways that are polar opposites: we either never see the family again, or we get a beautiful card or letter, letting us know they are still doing well. And sometimes there they are, in the back of the court, not as cases but as welcome visitors. And that is the best of all.

37

The Parents Who Have Money
to Burn on Hatred

Some of my worst cases happen when a family law case, a dissolution, bleeds into my dependency court. I use the word "bleed" advisedly, although physical and emotional wounds are the impetus. This man and woman, who loved each other once, forget that the opposite of love is indifference, or bittersweet regret, and commence to hate each other with the same passion that started the relationship and produced the kids in question. Oh, to be a material asset, incapable of emotion, fated to sit on either the mother or father's mantle, or wall, or etagere. "Who cares," says the Picasso. "I like them both."

But that hatred, when it treats the kids like that Picasso, has a very different result. And when the children are so traumatized by the back and forth, the constant bickering, or, worse, when they become emotionally unable to handle the trauma, a teacher, or doctor, or a caring adult in the family, calls the Department of Children and Family Services, and a petition gets filed.

Sometimes the children are removed from both parents, sometimes from only one. However, the case that was presented to me immediately made me nauseous. I knew no one would give one inch, and all the decisions were mine. Notwithstanding the fact that all dependency proceedings are confidential, even if you are a movie or television personality, or you are in *People* magazine the week you are in court. For those cases, the public will hear some of the battles on television, or read about it in the tabloids, but cases of people who are not famous can be a judicial nightmare, featuring almost day-to-day wranglings and hearings as each parent goes for the legal jugular.

Mom and Dad were married for about sixteen years. They had three children, two girls and a boy. All the kids were smart and articulate. They lived with their mother, and visited with their father. The mother was considerably younger than the father; in fact, her mother was about his age. This became important, as grandmother and mother become a duo dedicated to ruining Dad's life. I didn't know why then, and I don't know why now. She did not seem angry, or vindictive. Just icy cold. She had told the Department that he was molesting one of the girls. We did forensic testing, had the child examined, and interviewed by a professional trained to interview young children. The child was five. She indicated that her father had not touched her, that her mom told her to say that, and she wasn't afraid of her daddy.

At the hearing, I strongly cautioned the mother about coaching the children, and indicated to her that a Family Code section held that false allegations of physical or sexual abuse could result in loss of custody, and monitored visits.

"I understand," she said.

Grandma, in the back, said nothing.

I was prepared to terminate the case, and send them back to the Family Court but then, right after the hearing, the mother took the child to a rape crisis center, and the little girl told them she was touched by her daddy and was afraid of him. Everyone returned to court. I watched the child in court run to her father and sit on his lap. While I know it is possible for molested children to still love the molesting parent, this did not look like that. In all, no matter what I said, she or the grandmother took that child, directly against my orders, to five more rape crisis centers in about a month.

117

In response, I awarded custody of all the children to the father, with monitored visits for the mother. Her bid to cut this man out of her life backfired in a most dramatic way.

Chloe was twelve-years-old, and the fighting between her wealthy parents each for sole custody caused a psychological condition in which she was completely paralyzed. There was no physical etiology. I placed her with her maternal grandmother. Slowly, over the next two years, she got better. Each time I tried more contact with her parents, both of whom she refused to even see, Chloe fell apart again. I was never successful in reuniting her with either parent but was able to provide a legal guardianship to her grandmother. She simply couldn't trust either of them.

From special needs kids, whose parents argue about if or what might be the problem, to arguments about allergies and allergy medicine that puts a child in the hospital, to wives who try to hire hitmen or plant drugs in the husband's car in full view of the mounted camera in the parking lot, some people will do anything to get custody of their children against the other parent.

And they don't care what asset gets broken in the process.

38

Mentally Ill Parents

While dealing with odd parents, and the parents with strange and exotic worldviews is a challenge, it pales in comparison when trying to deal with mentally ill parents. That was a skill all its own, and could take you places that can leave you frustrated and sad equally.

I was still an attorney when a case came in of a homeless woman, Ruby, who had a child in a toilet. Ruby did not know she was pregnant, just that she had to go to the bathroom. When the baby appeared, she must have said something, as someone heard her, and knocked on the stall. She opened the stall, and the baby was rescued. A petition was filed. I was appointed to represent the mother. Ruby was still unsure that she actually had a baby, but was very sweet and cooperative. I quite liked her. Ruby had a diagnosis, I discovered, of schizophrenia, but not paranoid, or violent. The problem with representing her was that she was homeless, foggy on any details, and, of course, not on her medications. There was actually a place for her to go, a specialized group of apartments, where she could live with the baby, with a nurse on the property, and a doctor to prescribe her meds. I set it all up, and set a hearing date. Ruby had an appointment with the housing people the day after the hearing. She was present for the hearing, with all her belongings. I started to argue most vociferously for the time to get her settled into her new place, and stable on her meds. As I argued, I noticed the judge was trying not to smile. I thought, "Wow, he is really impressed with my skills."

However, I was disabused of that ego boost when I felt a tap on my shoulder from the bailiff. I turned to find my client sound asleep and snoring on the table. I turned to the judge.

"Well, she is sleeping the sleep of the innocent. Your honor, I still think that..."

The judge just smiled and my client never showed up for her appointment. I never saw Ruby again.

More problematic were those mentally ill parents who either did not accept their diagnoses, or believed they were irrelevant to child-rearing. This was exasperated by the homelessness that often accompanied the untreated illness. To add to the problem, homeless women were prey, and often pregnancy occurred, as well as the fact that normal urges did not disappear with either homelessness or illness. It was not unusual to have a child of two homeless people, who may or may not be interested in the child enough to get stable.

I had one client, Alice, who lived under a bridge in what appeared to be a homeless haven. There were tents, outdoor couches, and a stream flowing by. Alice lived under the third tree on the left in the park. The daughter, Sky, was removed from her homeless parents when there was a raid on her enclave by the police. I represented her, and a friend represented Jerry, the father. They were not a couple any longer. Both were fairly lucid, and the diagnosis was mild paranoia for both of them. This was going to be easy. I worked on getting a section eight, low-cost apartment for Alice. My friend did the same for the Jerry. In six months, Alice had left three different apartments, and returned to the bridge. I had gotten Sky returned to her, only to have Sky removed twice more, while Alice had another child. Alice absolutely refused to live where there were walls, and a ceiling. She said she felt suffocated. Jerry, however, fared completely differently. He got help, medication, and an apartment, and after a year regained custody of their child. Jerry and Sky did well, as I was informed during the hearings on the second child who was never reunited with my client. Alice simply could not put her child's needs above her own.

I was appointed to represent Sondra, who was bipolar and used drugs to self-medicate. She was diagnosed as manic depressive, and she was a prime example. On her meds, she was lucid, caring, and very bright and easy to deal with. Off them, Sondra veered from suicidal to queen of the world in a day. I had, at that time, a listed home phone number so my clients could reach me at any time. One Saturday, I got a call from Sondra's father, who told me to try to call her doctor and get her hospitalized. According to him, she was "circling the gardener." This was not a euphemism, as hypersexuality is symptom of the manic state.

I called Sondra's doctor and was told she was not a danger to herself or others, but to stay in touch. I wondered how deep my duty lay in that situation. Her parents had given up. Her children were safe with the father, and it looked like that would be the end of it until the phone rang.

"Hello?" I answered.

"Get me my children back now!" Sondra screamed at me.

"Sondra, it's Saturday. There's no court. Why don't you come in..."

After the call, Sondra called back. I hung up. She called back. After twenty calls in twenty minutes, I took the phone off the hook. I was terrified that Sondra would find out where I lived, so I decided to go to a friend's house. When I returned and replaced the phone, there was a message from my phone service that Sondra had called enough to clog their line, and they would not be answering that line anymore. I called the operator and told her my story. Even though it was not a weekday, she was able to change my phone number, and delist it on the spot. I felt better.

On Monday, I went to the judge and asked to be relieved from the case. I had given Sondra notice, but she did not appear. The judge granted my request. Several weeks later, I was leaving the court and there Sondra was, driving up next to me in a truck. She leaned out the window and I thought for a minute she might have had a gun. Instead, she said she was on her meds, and thanked me for my representation. One week later, her new attorney told me she was off her meds again, and gone.

In my first year on the bench, I had a mother, Cass, who was developmentally delayed, paranoid schizophrenic, but somewhat stable on her meds, living in a halfway house for life. She had a child, Britney, who was living with her grandfather. Cass came to the house every day, held and read to her child, and played with her. Cass could not regain custody, however. At the final parental rights hearing, the Department recommended termination of parental rights. The standard for that was that the child was adoptable by clear and convincing evidence, and here we had a grandparent ready to take that responsibility on, and there were no exceptions which would preclude the termination. There were several exceptions, but the one most often used was the exception that asked the court to find that the relationship between the parent and child was one which was so strong, that to sever it, would cause detriment to the child. It is a huge burden to overcome.

Did the parent visit regularly?

Remember birthdays and holidays?

Help with schoolwork?

Go to doctor appointments?

In short, did the parent act not like a friendly visitor to the child's life, but as a willing participant in the parenting of the child?

I looked at what Cass had done. What it took to get to her father's home day after day. How she was able to reach her child, even though it would not be long before her child's reading ability was beyond her.

How her child felt safe in the arms of her mother and was tucked in each night. She could not live outside the halfway house, but in my opinion, she had fulfilled the requirements of the exception.

With this case, I granted a legal guardianship with the grandfather, and left Cass's rights intact. I supposed the grandfather would never have stopped Cass from seeing her child, Britney, but I have never regretted that decision.

39

For Us, It's a Moment in Time...
For Juvie Kids, It's a Life Sentence

So, the allegations were pretty serious. Mom, mother of two teenage boys, had mental health issues. She was angry, volatile, and unpredictable. She was out of control both physically and verbally with the kids and her elderly parents.

We became alerted to this family because an incredible incident occurred over St. Patrick's Day weekend. In a fit of anger, Mom got up from the dinner table, stormed to the kitchen, seized the homemade Irish Soda bread, and bashed it over her father's head. The moment sent shockwaves throughout the house, and following that turbulent dinner, a concerned call was made, and a petition was filed.

The family was in court: grandparents, great-grandmother, both boys, Dad of the younger boy, and Mom. The Dad of the older boy was unknown, according to Mom. The older boy was with the grandparents, while the younger one was with his Dad.

We conducted the preliminaries, and as I recounted some of the petition and made my findings, Mom was appropriate and well-behaved. She was respectful to the court, quiet, and understanding of the rulings. I detained the older boy with his grandparents, and the younger one was released to Dad. I ordered an evaluation of Mom and set the next dates.

After this point, her attorney asked if his client could make a short statement to the court. I said yes, and off she went. Up from her lap came a huge file, filled with who knows what, all waved at me, accompanied by louder and louder completely non-understandable speech. The kids shook their heads, having been subjected to this their entire lives. As Mom transitioned from blaming her kids to targeting her parents, the poor kids shook their heads no. Parents with no filter or ability to care for anyone but themselves do not necessarily suffer from mental illness. Unfortunately, medications for some folks, like Mom here, are mostly useless. Families endure years of trying to appease them, walking on eggshells. Maybe you know someone like this? They believe they are Oscar-winning parents when they are beyond debilitating to their kids. They are never wrong and never silent. Anyway, we were all in the labor and delivery part of the mom's rant.

After twenty-five years on the bench, did I lose my mind for a second!?! Yep. Did I know better? Yep. Should I have told her nicely to save her comments for a trial? Yep.

She was now screaming uncontrollably. Time for the bailiff to intervene. Nope. I told my reporter to go off the record and told Mom she was no longer being recorded. Didn't help. Next step, I got off the bench and left the courtroom. She was then escorted out of the court, yelling all the way.

Did I know better? I did. Mental illness or just off, this Mom was never going to accept treatment or any help that required her to admit a problem. Luckily, in this case, we have family able and willing to provide care for these kids. Unluckily, when I am long gone from this case, the family will not be. Never-ending.

40

There's Never an Excuse for Physical Abuse

The family was not from America, and they had very specific family expectations for their teenaged daughter. They found out that their teenaged daughter was dating a "white kid," meaning an American boy, which also meant he was not of the same religion or traditions. They were appalled, and frightened, and they responded by beating the child so badly that she had to go to the hospital. The doctor immediately contacted the hospital social worker, who talked to the girl. She gave different answers than her parents for her injuries. Neither side said anything about physical abuse. The social worker determined that the injuries were abuse, and refused to allow the girl to return home. The Department went out to the home and removed the other child, a boy, from the home as well. The Department filed a petition, alleging physical abuse, and the family appeared before me in court.

They argued several issues, including a denial that they hit their daughter, and that even if they did, they were entitled to, as that is how they discipline children in their country, and that the boy had not been injured, so he needed to be returned home, as he was not in danger. Since the boy, also a teenager, believed that the discipline against his sister was reasonable, I disagreed. I mentioned that in America it was not appropriate to hit your children, and asked if they were open to other methods. The mother said yes, the father said no one had the right to tell him how to raise his children. I begged to disagree, and asked for safe relatives who might take the children during the case.

The grandmother, Yaya, stepped forward. She did not speak much English, and had spent much time wringing her hands. She promised to care for the children, and to not allow them to have unmonitored contact with their parents. I detained the children with her, and allowed contact so that the parents could drive the kids home to get their things, and then back to Yaya's.

Two days later, we were back in court. Yaya, bless her heart, had returned the children immediately to the parents. This time, I got an interpreter in court. I carefully explained what she had done wrong. Did she understand what I meant when I said the parents could not have unmonitored visits with the children? Wringing her hands, she assured me she did. I allowed her to keep the kids, and set the next date. Two days later, we were back in court. Guess why? Oh yes. Yaya, bless her heart, had returned the children to the parents as soon as she left court.

This time, I had no choice. I told her I could not return the children to her. She began to wring her hands and plead with me. This time would be different, she said. When I told her I could not trust her word, she began to wail. Then, clunk, over Yaya went, in a dead faint.

The paramedics came, took Yaya, and eventually Dad got the seriousness of the situation. He then followed the case plan on getting his kids back, which he did.

41

The Indian Child Welfare Act (ICWA)

For sixteen years, I presided over the only state-designated Indian court in the country other than Tribal Courts, which were separate from any state court system. Everywhere else, if an Indian child was taken into dependency, the case went to whatever court was in the rotation. Years before I got there, Los Angeles decided to dedicate one court to all Indian cases, and also designated a separate Indian social worker unit to service those cases. I believed that to be a smart decision for a number of reasons, and was happy to inherit that court when I was hired as a referee. A referee and/or commissioner is a subordinate bench officer. They are usually only in certain courts. They have exactly the same power as a judge, but their decisions can be rechecked by a judge if requested by a party—a rare event.

There is a completely separate Federal Act that deals with Indian children, called the Indian Child Welfare Act (ICWA). A few years ago, it was codified and added to the State Welfare and Institutions Code. The Act adds an overlay of protection to the removal of Indian children from their homes. Most families who foster or adopt are Caucasian because they represent over 60 percent of the general population. The number of Indian children who were removed and absorbed by Caucasians is historical, ongoing, and the impetus for ICWA existing.

To be eligible for ICWA, the tribe must be Federally recognized. The child must be a member of the tribe under eighteen years of age, or have a parent who is a member of the tribe, or simply, the tribe indicates the child is eligible. Some tribes allow membership up to three generations, some less.

I loved that part of the court. I had a real affinity for the Indian community, and a firm commitment to the concept of Indian sovereignty. I got along well with the Indian specialist attorneys and generated several forms we used in our court to assure Tribal rights, contacts, and future involvement. One day, I had a visit from some Tribal representatives from an out-of-state tribe. I welcomed them into my chambers and regaled them with how I felt about ICWA, how I ran the court, how I...well, I went on and on. I repeatedly asked if they had any questions for me. No one said a word. After they left, I asked my Indian expert what had happened.

She said, "Your honor, Indians do not speak, out of respect, until the other person stops speaking. And, your honor, you never really stopped talking!"

Oops. Well, I learned a real lesson then, not only about Indians, but about how to behave with our Indian children, who would look sullen in foster care, by not speaking at all. I felt this cultural characteristic was something our foster families needed to know, and wrote a short list of Indian beliefs and behaviors to give to foster parents.

ICWA is a very controversial act. It confers rights of one group of children that are not conferred on any other. No other racial or ethnic group has the same rights as Indian children. With our usual children, we are required to look at appropriate relatives before placing children outside the family. If there are no relatives, there is no impediment to the type of family for placement, and eventually, possible adoption. But if the child is Indian, the court must make specific findings, as the burden of proof is on the right of the tribe to first take placement of the child, or find someone in the tribe to take the child.

What complicates matters is that many of our children are mixed race. They are half, quarter Indian, and had not identified as Indian. They were removed from homes where Indian parents had long been gone, or were not tribe affiliated. They were living with values different from those espoused by Indian tribes, and frankly, not all tribes should be lumped together. Indian tribes have different lifestyles, and past enmities. Gaming tribes have resources that other tribes do not have. Some tribes have few members, some many. Los Angeles has more Indian tribes than anywhere else in California. However, there are no reservations, and all groups are considered urban in character. Therefore, group assistance is not afforded to those relatives who live in a group environment.

The problem with ICWA is a national problem. Indians who are impoverished rely on state services for a child that the tribe could not take care of during the dependency process. Even so, our ICWA mandate is to make sure all Indian children are placed, whenever possible, in Indian homes.

Even with stricter laws protecting Indian children, the lack of Indian foster homes, local relatives, or lack of Tribal intervention, means that most of these children are not in Indian homes. Here is the problem with that. Our Indian children are adopted in non-Indian homes. That does not make them no longer Indian. And we see that many years later, with Indian adults reclaiming their heritage by coming back to their tribes.

I participated in hundreds of placements for these children, and have tried my best to honor the spirit of ICWA. I have failed more than I wanted, especially when the final adoptive family clearly would not raise the child in Indian ways. But my mandate was to make sure this child, as all others, had a safe and stable childhood. I hoped it helped, and that their spirits were strong and able to finally be at peace.

42

Problems Native American Children Face

One of the major problems with Native American children is the distance of the court from the tribe. Since Los Angeles is an urban center, the actual tribal seat, which may or may not include a tribal court, is usually some distance from the child.

This is important because the tribe has a very difficult decision right from the start. If the child is removed to the tribe, the parent, still in Los Angeles, does not have access to that child for visitation and bonding and attachment purposes. Depending on the age of the child, that time together is crucial. But if the tribe waits to allow a parent to complete reunification, that child may have had up to almost two years to become part of the foster home placement.

When a lot of time passes, the issue is no longer focused on returning the child to the family of origin, but rather the child's best interest in long-term stability. And the standard for movement to the tribe, or anywhere other than the current home, is codified as requiring "good cause" to go outside the Indian home preference. Good cause is not defined in the law, other than case-by-case.

I had dozens of Indian cases, and little controversy. I made sure the tribes were noticed properly, allowed intervention where requested, and had their input each step of the way. All Federally recognized tribes have the right to intervene in any dependency case involving one of the tribe's children. This is done by a telephone call to the court or, usually, by written request. The tribe becomes a separate party to the case, with all the rights attached for reports, trial, witnesses. Sometimes the parents and tribe disagree about placement, and each gets a say equal to the other.

Sandro was born to a drug-addicted mother, in 1998. The mother was one half Chippewa, and the father was one half Navajo. The tribes were notified. Neither tribe intervened or appeared in any way, until the six-month review hearing. The Chippewa nation appeared and said the child was Indian, but did not have an adoptive home for the child. The child was placed at three months with non-Indian foster parents, with whom he remained throughout the rest of the proceedings.

If they wished, they could ask to transfer the entire case to Minnesota, as the Act states that, "On petition of either parent, child, or Indian tribe, state court proceedings for foster care placement, or termination of parental rights of an Indian child, must be transferred to the tribal court unless good cause exists, either parent objects, or the tribe declines jurisdiction. If transfer does not occur, the matter remains in state court." The prerequisite is that the tribe have an actual tribal court to accept the transfer. I had many transfers go very well, and many cases where the non-Indian parent objects to transfer, which effectively stops it. In this case, the tribe waited to see if the mother could regain custody of Sandro. She did not, and in September, 1999, reunification services were terminated, and the case set for permanency. The tribe then said they had identified a cousin of the mother who would adopt the child.

The Chippewa nation did not move to transfer. The cousin, at some point soon thereafter, said she wanted the child to stay with the foster parents. I had initiated a dialogue between the tribe and foster parents, hoping Sandro got some resolution everyone could live with.

In March of 2000, the Band of Indians to which the mother belonged, within the larger category of Chippewa Tribe, moved to intervene. In May, they requested the child be placed on the reservation with newly found adopted relatives. I set the matter for trial.

I ordered an expert familiar with Indian ethnology, as required by law, to interview all parties, and render an opinion as to the detriment to remove the child from his two-year home, and place them with his Indian relatives. My stance was ICWA still trumped non-ICWA, as keeping your roots should be one less concern later on for adopted children. But I was willing to hear all sides, especially from the experts. The father was never involved. The mother was peripherally involved now that the Department had an opinion, but she was willing to abide by mine. However, the child's counsel was adamantly opposed removal from the current foster home. The foster parents were adamant that they wanted to adopt. Foster dad was fifty-years-old and the foster mom was forty-three. They had grown children and grandchildren.

The Indian expert gave her opinion that the child could be removed and replaced without trauma. The child's expert said that removal would be a severe trauma, and a disrupted attachment associated with multiple emotional and psychological problems in the future.

The foster parents had attained de facto parent status, which gave them limited rights in the case, including the right to have a privately hired attorney present to argue for them. They hired an attorney who said in court, "[The foster parents'] greatest wish is to maintain contact with the tribe. They would be willing to travel to Minnesota to take the child. They recognize the value of the culture and seek only to reinforce it."

The foster father testified in Spanish, his language of origin, through an interpreter. I got no hint that he was the least bit aware, or interested, in the Indian heritage of this child.

My decision was to place the child for adoption with the tribal relatives in Minnesota. This stay was requested, and denied. Sandro's counsel sought a writ to stay the removal of the child. It was granted by the appellate court. Sandro would stay in California pending the appeal of my decision. I knew where this was going.

Out of the thousands of cases I've ruled on, I have certainly been reversed. Two of my cases went to the California Supreme Court, who affirmed my original decision. This was not one of them.

Indian cases have all kinds of constitutional flavors, and published cases are apt to have a variety of opinions at odds with other jurisdictional opinions.

I was reversed in July of 2001. The court graciously found that I "felt compelled" by the act to remove the child. They found under a subsequently discredited theory that pursuant to the "existing Indian family doctrine," the mother had virtually no contact with the tribe in adulthood, and the child therefore had no existing Indian family. The relationship was so attenuated as to constitute good cause to override ICWA. The case had been taken up to the Supreme Court, where two justices voted to hear it, but were outvoted by the majority. Sandro stayed with his foster parents. If he ever had any contact with the tribe, I never heard about it.

Sandro is an adult now. I hope he is happy.

43

Domestic Violence Is Rampant in Juvie Cases

Do you know how moss impacts a tree in the tropics? In bits and pieces, the moss slowly takes over the tree until it dies. If you think about it, domestic violence relationships operate the same way.

First there is a little criticism, not much, but just enough to make someone feel a little nervous. Then slowly, the criticism gets worse, and the self-esteem begins to erode. Then, at some point, the hitting starts. Then the beating, and then, in worst-case scenarios, children are ordered or indoctrinated to join in. This scenario can be either the man or woman in the household as I've seen it both ways.

If the woman or man chooses to leave, because of fear and indoctrination, the children will refuse to go. They identify with and stay with the person with the power. And, if things have moved far enough, she or he will never get to leave. There will be murder.

When I worked as a judge, the statistics were terrible. I just hated ruling in those cases. I was torn between anger at the perpetrator and anger at the victim. I wanted to shout at the top of my lungs to the victims, both male and female, "Get out! Take our help. Send him or her to jail! Stop making his bail, stop taking him or her back, stop putting your kids in danger."

In my day, I came across so many parents who just did not understand the effects their behaviors had on their own children. I took classes that show that even hearing arguments in another room affects the brains of children as young as newborn. They do not learn the same as children not affected. It also takes time to restructure the fight or flight response, which takes over most of their developing brain. It is a scourge, and it does not help that the judicial fix and the therapeutic fix are diametrically opposed. Judicial wants to separate the family and be punitive, whereas therapeutic wants the family together and working through their problems. I want those kids safe. I want them out of that house. I want them as far away as possible from the abused parent who will not go to a shelter yet again. The abused parent who shows up with bruises all over and says he or she fell down the stairs yet again.

From hearing many domestic abuse cases over the years, there was a pattern I recognized. Domestic violent cases tended to be made of young, impoverished couples. These couples had early problems that led to the first-time fisticuffs. They tended to have not learned to use their words to express their stress and frustrations. They then had a first baby, which contributed to their financial burdens. Stress was the common denominator with these families, but we as a system and society can help them by offering services, general encouragement, and support as well as address the causes of their frustrations. It must be said that I was always so heartened when a victim and/or a perp accepted the help offered to them. The theory of domestic violence calls for treatment in three ways:

1. A batterer program where a batterer learns why they are violent.
2. A victims program that helps them with their self-esteem, gets them to safety, and rebuilds their life.
3. If the family is still intact, even though living separately, and have completed their respective programs, then family therapy may be ordered.

Then there were the families where the violence was more entrenched. Regular abuse, over years, involving law enforcement.

Economic burdens also a reoccurring issue. For a woman, where would she go? The husband was the major breadwinner. How would she support her kids? Would he be the one to get custody, as he promised her would happen if she left? Those cases were harder to work with, but possible, with community support, a supportive extended family, and serious oversight. It brought me so much joy when I saw a woman come out stronger, tougher, working, and in charge of her life for the first time in many years. I had seen batterers of both sexes confront their own childhood trauma, and fight their way out to become different people. It was beyond miraculous when those successful families never returned to court.

But there were those, mostly men, who simply did not intend to listen to anyone. They were not scared by court, the police, or anything else. Why? Because they were willing to die to keep doing what they were doing. The women and children who belonged to them, they were chattel, and there was no way to stop them. To the victims of such men, and some women, I would tell them, "You must move away and change your name." I meant it. Those types of abusers would use the children as pawns, and continued battering on another front.

One such case included a woman named Gina. She was very young with a new baby, and her husband was much older, and in jail for assaulting her. Gina had the baby in a shelter, and I asked her a question in front of her husband.

"Do you want to move away from the front seats, and over to the very back of the court, so he could not talk to you?"

The husband gave me a look. I ignored it. I could always tell so much by the victim's answer when I asked that question. In this case, Gina quickly nodded.

"Thank you," she said before running to the back. She already had a restraining order.

That day, I proceeded to go over the first hearing and I asked the husband if he understood what the restraining order meant. He refused to answer me. I asked again, no contact, in person, on the phone, in writing, on social media. I told him we would sit there until he answered. He finally, with head down, acknowledged that he understood. I recessed the hearing. He stood up to be taken back to his cell. I turned my head, and he turned and looked at her, yelling at her, "I'm sorry, baby, I blacked out!" I ordered him removed immediately. She looked stricken. He had no intention of following that restraining order. She is at highest risk, even with the new baby, a confidential placement, and him in jail.

"If you see something, say something" is a new byword. For these cases, it is imperative to always speak up.

44

Not So Handsome

As the Eagles song says, he was "brutally handsome." This man I speak of bore a strong resemblance to Scott Peterson. His name was not Scott. Here, I'll call him "Mr. Handsome" and I remembered heads turning as he swaggered into the courtroom, which was not easy as his hands and legs were in chains. He was placed in the seat we use for prisoners. He was big, arrogant, and angry.

I couldn't stand him on sight.

Usually, petitions for domestic violence were a few paragraphs per incident, but Dean's petition took up a full page with detailed bruises, cuts, contusions, scratches, and multiple broken bones. He had beaten his wife, Suzie, within an inch of her life. The police had been called when her father came to visit and found her nearly dead. He took his unresponsive daughter to the hospital. She had survived, barely, and she stood in court accompanied by her father. Suzie was around five feet tall, and maybe weighed eighty-five pounds soaking wet.

Suzie stared resolutely at me, as Mr. Handsome called out to her.

"Suzie. Suzie! I love you, baby. I'll be coming home to you soon. I promise, baby."

I pounded my gavel. "Mr. ——! One more word out of you, and I'll have you removed from the court and have your lawyer fill you in."

Mr. Handsome shot me a look. He was angry. "You know, Judge, I have a constitutional right to free speech..." and blah, blah, blah.

I had had enough of this. I addressed the bailiff. "Get him out of here."

That order got Mr. Handsome's attention.

"Okay, okay. I'll be quiet," he said, looking at Suzie, who continued to stare at me.

You see, batterers can't stand not being in control, even if it's an illusion. Being removed from the court would have put him, in his mind, out of control of the situation.

For juvenile court proceedings involving the welfare of a child, the procedure begins at an initial hearing, or detention hearing. Then I make detention orders, where the children will be detained pending the next hearing, and seek services to get the family started on reunification. This time, however, was different. I read into the record every word of the petition. Every word. I looked straight at Mr. Handsome as I did it.

"Petitioner states the Respondent slammed her onto the kitchen floor whereby Respondent sat on Petitioner's torso and proceeded to punch her multiple times in the left eye socket and left jaw. Respondent then grabbed the Petitioner by the neck to obstruct airway as blood poured out of Petitioner's mouth..."

Mr. Handsome smirked at me, and actually flexed a bit as he got comfortable in his seat. As I continued to read every gory detail of the damage he had done, he sat up and protested loudly.

"Your honor, this is a bunch of crap! Suzie would never say all this."

She and the hospital personnel recorded every bruise. I also read into the record Mr. Handsome's prior history, which included jail time for assault against a former girlfriend, and child endangerment against the baby he had with her. In this petition there were two children, ages two and one. When he came to argue regarding temporary placement of the children, Suzie's lawyer asked for the children to be returned to the mother, as the father was in custody. I looked at Suzie.

"If he were released tomorrow, would he return home?"

Suzie looked at me. "It's his home. He could return if he wanted."

I tried not to sigh. I immediately turned my attention to Suzie's father.

"Can you take custody of the children and protect them?"

Suzie's father nodded. "Yes, your honor, I can do that."

I ordered no contact for the father, and monitored visits for the mother. I also stipulated that if the father got out of custody before the next hearing, the mother's visits had to be in the Department office, in case they together strong-armed grandfather and kidnapped the children. I also ordered a battered women class for her, and a batterer class for him, and set the next date.

Later, I woke up at three o'clock in the morning. I sat bolt upright in bed, thinking what a fool I was. I couldn't believe what I had done. Being new on the bench was no excuse. I had asked a question of a battered woman in front of the batterer! Why had I done that!?! Common sense should have prevailed, and experience. My only thought was I had been so angry with him, I lost my focus, and put her, and the kids, in jeopardy if he got out.

Since that hearing, I made some changes on how to conduct domestic violence proceedings. For one, I never again, at any time, asked the direct question of a battered woman from the bench. Instead, I allowed the lawyers to argue the safety issues, so as to shield their clients from making personal statements. I also separated the men and women, depending on who did the battering, with the victim in front and batterer behind, so they would not have to confront their aggressor eye to eye. I also had the victim leave first, and sometimes had my bailiff escort them to their cars, to make sure there was no confrontation. But batterers are insidious, and their ways to meet are numerous, especially at the beginning of freedom, when the victim is most vulnerable. I also made it a point to order no social media contact, no telephone contact, no in-person contact. I issued restraining orders. But despite all my efforts to protect victims, there were times when the batterer would appear in church, at a relative's birthday party, at the supermarket, at the train station. For those times, arrests were minimal, and time served was never long.

It was always dispiriting to see these cases play out the way they did.

Domestic violence is a complicated dance, likened to the French Apache dance, where the sailor and streetwalker dance to her death. A true batterer cannot be stopped, and it takes the victim years to regain lost self-esteem and freedom from fear. In Suzie's case, it worked out. Most of the time, sadly, it does not.

With Suzie, however, there was a happier ending. Mr. Handsome eventually got sixty-five years in prison because of all his priors. Suzie also completed her classes and regained custody of her children. After reunification, I checked each reporting record to make sure she did not telephone, write, or visit him.

She never did.

45

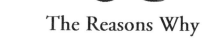

The Reasons Why
Victims Stay with Their Abusers

"I feel like a wilted rose with my petals
falling off one at a time."

—One Domestic Violence Victim

My heart broke hearing the above statement from a woman whose kids were removed due to domestic violence (DV) by the father of her youngest child. I was struck by the beauty and sadness of that description. I asked her if I could repeat what she said when I spoke to groups about domestic violence, and she graciously agreed. I often spoke to DV groups, and it hurt my soul to see such pain in their eyes. The abuse they've endured, the memories that their brains and bodies hold. I saw these women and men as beautiful entities who shed one piece of self-esteem each time their partner verbally or physically goes at them. Finally, only the stem is left. But that stem, if rooted properly, can regrow and regenerate.

I wanted my work to be water for that stem.

Our job at Juvie and social services was to nurture, feed, and carefully protect that new growth, starting with getting the abuser out of the home. Sometimes it was surprisingly easy, as abusers were excellent at looking docile and cooperative around others who were not afraid of them. They wanted to make a good impression to the court and the victim, and also be in the, "I'm so sorry. I love you. I'll never do that again. I'll change," stage. This stage always emerged during the small window of opportunity there was to serve them with a restraining order in court.

Of course, abiding by the restraining order, when granted, was another matter. As the anger gripped them again, restraining orders meant little. They would begin to stalk again, and many victims were not yet strong enough to resist. They needed more time to grow.

Domestic violence starts almost at birth. The winnowing begins. Boys who witnessed domestic violence are ten times more likely to embrace some form of it themselves. They may even be encouraged to join in, or be ordered to, and too frightened to resist, so they join the oppressor. Girls are marginalized, isolated, alienated, brainwashed, and sometimes drugged out, as their mothers, to escape the fear and pain.

I have had grandmothers tell me that their sons did nothing wrong, that the job of the mother was to keep the peace and keep a well-run household. Religious leaders of all persuasions exhort women to bow down to their men, as he is the head and she is the heart of the family.

Heartsore, heartbroken, or just plain broken, these people were unable to believe that they could make it alone. That they had any worth at all. After all, they were told in every way, every day, that their partner was the only one who could or would ever care for them. In turn, these victims cannot fathom making a living, moving out, starting over. Their abuser had made sure of it by removing any and all support from the lives of the victims. Like a cheetah cutting the lame wildebeest from the herd, these people know where the emotionally lame people are. With laser-like focus, they could pick out vulnerable partners in a room full of strangers.

People unfamiliar with the domestic violence culture cannot understand the plight of the victims, and thus have no empathy. I can just hear the...

"Why don't they just leave?"

"There are shelters, you know."

"Just call the police."

"Go to a relative or friend's home."

"I wouldn't put up with that for a minute!"

"If he/she ever talked to me like that, treated me like that, hit me like that, well, he/she would be plenty sorry."

Yes, I hear you. So do the victims, by the way. Picture, if you will, a mountain by the sea. Every day, water laps against the mountain. Every minute of every day. Eventually the mountain wears down, is carved to fit where the water hits it. It starts with loving attention, some recommendations for adjusting some lifestyle choice, perhaps clothing, speech, manners. Then come the insults. Then the threats. Then the physical violence. And your behavior comports to the "learned responses" you need to stay alive. And, of course, maybe this time he means it. He will kill you.

Now picture your status in the community, and even in your family. Do you want to tell them? Wouldn't you be embarrassed? Mortified? Do you know where to live, how to get a job, where to find childcare? Do you have to tell the school, to keep the abuser away? Do you have to move your kids to another school, where he can't find you? He controls the money. You don't have any.

To get away takes courage. I am in awe of the women, especially those with children, who can do it. I'm in awe of the men who stop looking at their partners and children as their property, and learn to look at them as human beings. I am in awe of the boys who do not become batterers, of the girls who do not become some other man's property.

My job was to get that rose blooming.

46

Some Parents Need to Be Raised Again

It was the beginning of a new day. I did a calendar call. I went through each case with the lawyers to set up the day. Trials get set in the afternoons from shortest to longest. Case reviews get done first; the rest go when they are ready. I had read all the review reports from the Department, with the lawyer and social worker recommendations. Return, no return, parents were in compliance with their case plans, parents had done nothing on their case plans, parents had compiled somewhat. Mom was great, Dad blew. Dad was great, Mom was in the wind. And I tried to remember always that these were human beings underneath all the horror and poor judgment. There were reasons you could pinpoint that got them there in my court.

So I think my job was to acknowledge the reasons for why they were the way they were and kind of cheerlead these parents by hoping enthusiastically that they would make the necessary changes to regain custody of their children, and start over. I commented on those parents who had themselves come through the system and were repeating the cycle with their own children. I told one young man who had started to use violence to control his younger wife, that I knew he had been through the same, and to look at the face of his newborn baby, and picture where he wanted that baby to be when he was the age of his father. I told him I'd be helping him heal from his own pain, as if he was the child before me, so as to stop the cycle. I explained why he could not move back in with the mother, who had retained the child in her custody, until I was assured he could parent and partner without anger, violence, or control. I told him I know he could do it. After saying all this, hoping this young man heard me, he instead responded with bewilderment and anger.

"This is my family!" he said. "They need to be with me."

I repeated my decision calmly, but clearly.

"I will not listen to any more justifications or excuses. My decision is final."

With that, the young man finally nodded at me, and I nodded back. He got it.

Another domestic violence case has stayed with me. Her name was Rita. Rita had come through horrible domestic violence. The father of her children beat her so badly she had to be hospitalized. But there Rita was standing in front of me, ready to get her kids back. I congratulated her and she smiled. The Department of Children and Family Services (DCFS) was ready to close the case, but then I saw that the father had done absolutely nothing.

He was, however, still in town, and visiting the children!?! She was not monitoring those visits. I became worried. The kids' father had controlled Rita for years. I had hoped the battered women's group had worked, and she knew what she must do. I told her that the father was a great big spider just waiting in his web for her to get out of the system before he oozed back into her life. There was a restraining order, but little family support, and no social worker checking on this family. Sometimes, my gut told me not yet, she wasn't ready yet, not today. Either I trusted her, or I went against the DCFS' recommendations and kept the case open indefinitely. I closed her case. I then showed her my crossed fingers, that we wouldn't see her or her children again. She smiled, and promised. She was right. I didn't.

All my job required me to do was listen to the lawyers argue, and render a decision. Talking directly to the parents, explaining, was not really my job. But I thought, in Juvie, the parents were not just perpetrators, they were part of the system as a whole. When there was buy-in, and agreement, they did better.

I was big on predicting success. Big on finding the best that I could in a situation.

But I was also very direct and clear. At least that was what they told me. In letters, and from the relatives in the back of the courtroom. One grandfather told me the family called me "the little bulldog." Their children left my courtroom with no confusion as to what I wanted, and what would happen if I didn't get it. We laughed, but the kids in those cases got it together. Many more times, they didn't. In the system, I was no more to be trusted than any other person.

Juvie was bewildering, complex, difficult—besides the legal mumbo-jumbo, there was the Department of Children and Family Services and its social workers, and nonprofit or religious community providers, all with their own set of rules. It was not unusual to have kids in several different homes, even with relatives, and no transportation. It was a daunting task, and the parents were impaired in many ways. These parents didn't have jobs, but they had drug addictions they had to kick. They had little to no support from estranged families, housing problems, money problems, life problems. In other words, these parents needed to be re-raised themselves. Like Belinda.

Belinda had a drug problem. She also was physically abusive against her kids, all five of them under the age of ten. She had a husband with a degenerative disease. She was about thirty and looked about fifty, and she weighed about ten pounds. When I saw her in court, she was sober, she had taken all the classes, and the kids were all in school and doing well. Her husband was there, on a cane, looking gaunt and unwell. DCFS wanted to close the case. I did not. I did not yet trust this family not to implode again.

"Belinda, a few things need to happen before your children can return to you. First, I will be sending a public health nurse out to set up respite for you. I am ordering that you take one hour each week and leave the house. Take a walk, get your nails done, see a friend."

Belinda made eye contact with me. "Your honor, I cannot imagine doing that." She then started to cry.

"Belinda, you must. You cannot take care of that family without relapsing unless you start taking care of yourself."

I knew that even if Belinda went to a 12-step program, no matter how well it worked, it was, in fact, more work. That mother of five had her hands full and needed some joy in her life. Something that had no intrinsic worth at all other than pure fun. I kept the case open for six more months. No one objected. Then we closed the case.

Our judicial responsibility was to make good on our promises to help the parents become better. To re-educate, re-train, and polish while remembering at all times that we must protect the children first. The problem was, frequently, who did the parenting?

47

When Children Give Testimony

O ne of the more interesting aspects of Juvie is just where we get our information. We rely on mandated reporters such as teachers and therapists for more reliable reporting. Angry and frightened relatives who call the child abuse hotline are also a source of information. They are relatives who have had enough of parents who are abusive to their nieces and nephews or grandchildren, and want the children protected by getting legal custody through the courts. Neighbors are next, some have gone even so far as to tape the yelling, slapping, throwing, and screaming coming from the next door apartment before calling the police. While the parents rant and rave about how these neighbors have always been out to get them, we listen to the tape. In one case, we heard the three-year-old girl yelling at the father to stop hitting mommy.

Bad divorces regularly breed calls. Mom accused Dad of abuse or molesting their child, Dad did the same to the mom or her new boyfriend. All of this left us with a he said/she said, and we tried to parse out who, if anyone, was telling the truth. Oftentimes we wondered just how did these people ever get together in the first place?

Grandma calls weekly to complain about the mother. Maternal Aunt calls regularly to complain about the father. And so on, and on, and on. Paternal Grandmother never saw the father, her son, touch "that whore," the kids' mother, even as that "whore's" family line up to recount beating after beating. But the most poignant information and testimony was always the testimony from the children themselves.

Questioning children is a delicate endeavor. How do we question them in an unbiased way? How do we sort out testimony from a three-year-old, a five-year-old, or a seven-year-old with developmental disabilities? Therapists differ about the reliability of testimony. There are dozens of groundbreaking studies which quantify the ability of children to see, understand, relate, and remember. My friend, also at Juvie, decided to run her own study with her three-year-old granddaughter, Nancy. She asked her if she had enjoyed her visit to the zoo.

Nancy said, "Yes, I did."

My friend asked her if she liked the fluffy pink bunny she got at the zoo?

Nancy said, "Yes, I did."

But you see, there was no zoo and no bunny. Just a little girl who loved her grandmother and wanted to please her by agreeing with her questions.

Oy.

Most professionals could ask children to recount without coaching or suggesting the answers. The questions were open ended, and did not require just a "yes" or "no" answer. The "did your daddy touch you" was a question never asked anymore. Of course he did. Hugs, baths, even being potty trained, there were lots of times daddy touches his kids. We had gotten far more sophisticated over time, and could rely more and more on the reliability of the testimony.

Conversely, we heard that young children did not lie because they had not learned yet that there were consequences for lying, or there was a need to lie. They always just told the truth.

Ask Nancy.

There was one case where the dad wasn't allowed back in the house. But Mom let him back in. The five-year-old told the social worker when she came out of her room, she saw that Daddy was spending the night. When confronted, the mom admitted yes, but that was months ago, before the order was made for him to vacate the family home. The older children agreed with Mom. Dad said the same. How to get to the truth here? Can we ask the five-year-old "when?" No, because that was too abstract. Sometimes we went by holidays, before or after Thanksgiving, near Christmas, birthday parties. Around seven or so, the ability to recount and clarify time was pretty good for most kids. But by then, they also know that bad things may happen to Mommy or Daddy if the truth is revealed, and either the child didn't want to talk at all, or hedged what they told the teacher, or worker. Or they would recant completely, and take responsibility for the family by saying they lied, which was more than likely not true.

Then there were times when yes, the children did lie. Teenaged girls who wanted Mom's new boyfriend out of the house would allege molest. And some of those girls who really were molested would blackmail the molester for clothes, phones, or even a car. So, by the time the case got to court, we had a pretty unlikable witness called a liar by both parents.

Siblings, afraid of being separated or removed, have turned on each other, and contradict the reporting sibling. There have been instances where a sibling would call another sibling a liar, and deny all the abuse going on in the home.

I have had seen it all in Juvie. Coaching by parents or relatives, and finally, a psychological condition known as "folie à deux," which is a mental disorder that two people share and experience at the same time, usually affecting members of a close family. Folie à deux is rare, and happened when the children's safety was completely bound up in a parent. The parent would make up an accusation, and the children would back up that accusation 100 percent. Even if it was impossible. I recall in one family; the mother accused the father of molesting both of their children. As the case developed, she accused the children's teachers, the doctor, even the mailman of molest. The children testified adamantly that this all happened, even though the most likely molester, the father, was residing in another state during the reporting period. He had abandoned the children to the mother, knowing she had mental health issues, and now wanted to regain some sort of custody. This was not going to happen because of the accusations. Even though the testimonies were blatantly false, I simply could not remove the children without a complete breakdown. So I took the testimonies and ordered visits for the father in a therapeutic setting, until the children could possibly be weaned away from the mother, which ended up happening slowly.

All our information came from every contact with the families, and the families themselves. Good or bad, we had to work with what we had. Finding needles in haystacks, slow and laborious, the truth invariably comes out. Of course, the truth emerges after the damage has been done. Finding the truth was the end for most trials; for Juvie it was only the beginning.

48

Do Judges Get Scared?

I am often asked about my feelings of safety. Am I fearful that my job, removing children from parents, puts me in jeopardy? Since I am the very face of the consequences, it is easier for parents to blame me than it is to blame themselves. Because of this, the common question I get is, "Aren't you scared?"

I find it an interesting question. After all, I am not the social worker, the one who is out there in the field, on the ground, walking into a hornet's nest with no protection, and leaving with the children amidst a firestorm. I am in a protected setting, with the bailiff by my side, after a thorough check of the families as they enter the front door of the courthouse.

We have had to evacuate the courtroom several times after bomb threats have been called in. We had a father stand-off with police in our courtyard, that went on from late afternoon until the early morning, and necessitated the bench to be evacuated from a hidden court location. Cars had to be left in the garage, and calls had to be made to get home and to work the next day. Our garage is accessible only with a special key card. However, and I have looked at this with some humor, just above our cars is a mesh wall up to which the family's cars are parked. It would not be a stretch to have a car of one of my cases parked directly above my car. The person in the car could wave to me through the mesh. Since these exchanges were before they entered the guarded courthouse and went through the metal detector, I fervently hoped they were not waving with a gun!

In our building, there was only one cafeteria. In some courthouses, the judges had a small private lunchroom, but not us. So, when I went to the cafeteria to get lunch, morning families that had just finished, and afternoon families I had not seen yet were all around me. Sometimes they greeted me with a smile, sometimes not. Sometimes I saw partners who, by virtue of the allegations, were not supposed to be together, or around the children, and who had sworn that in court. Yet there they were, happily having lunch together, or getting into a car together. I was obligated to report those violations from the bench when I heard the case.

Yeah, it was awkward.

Then there were our mental health parents. I had hidden behind a friend, and had friends do the same, as we negotiated lunch without being seen. Many judges brought lunch from home, and we all had the equivalent of a small kitchen in our chambers. But I liked to get out of the chambers for a breather, and if I was not lunching with a friend outside of the building, I would go to the cafeteria.

With all that, with all the fury that erupts in the courtroom, not one of us had ever been injured. I do know two of my friends who had police protection for several weeks after a threat, but that also resulted in nothing. I often wondered why. We were in such a volatile system.

I think, although I have no scientific basis for this, the families in crisis know the deal. That the worst domestic violence perpetrator is a bully and a coward and will not fight anyone with more authority than he has. That foreign families, where the man lords over it all, will not tackle the police. But most parents know they have messed up. They may not admit it, and fight it to the last breath, but in their hearts, they know they want better for their children. It was, however, a seriously loaded atmosphere. We were dealing with gang members, drug dealers, identity thefts on a national scale, besides our plain old screwed-up parents. Too young, too ignorant, too poor, too depressed, too much of too little, these parents were a threat only to themselves.

But there was this one time...

The child was about five. I don't recall the allegations, but I had to remove him from both parents. He was placed with his grandmother. Dad was a private investigator who was very unhappy and belligerent. He was also big. I mean really big. And verbal. Really verbal. I don't recall much about Mom, other than she was a bit of a cypher in the mix. We set the next hearing date and at that time, I released the boy to his father. He had done his programs, and made a good job of it.

Unfortunately, as was not unusual in our system, something went wrong, and I had to remove the child again. The child went back to his grandmother after a roaring trial by the father. As I headed home that night, musing on that specific case, I happened to look over at the truck driving next to me, and saw, with a shock, it was Mr. Private Investigator.

Uh-oh.

We proceeded to drive down the freeway, and took the same exit. He had private detected me! He knew where I lived and he was angry. Now I was scared. When I got home, I told my husband the private detective's name, and that if anything happened to me, to get the police to see him. I also described the truck and told my husband to watch out for it. Was I paranoid? Wouldn't you be?

The next day, I pulled that case file to get more information about him that I could lodge with my husband. I told my bailiff what had happened, and he filed a confidential report. Only later, as I calmed down, did I remember something I had stored away without comprehending. The emotional clouds parted and logic came into light. The child was with his grandmother, who lived in my city. Where the freeway exit would have taken him.

Oh dear. Mr. Private Investigator was visiting his son. Not to be thought a complete fool, I convinced myself he could do both, visit his son and come get me right after. It was better to be safe than sorry.

Several months later, I sent the child back to his dad, and closed the case. As Mr. Private Investigator stood to leave, he asked to address the court. I said he could.

He looked at me, then said, "I just want it to be known that you have always been fair to me and I want to thank you for doing your job. Thank you."

Tears welled up in my eyes. I responded.

"Thank you for saying that and thank you for putting your child's needs before your own."

He nodded and then left. I never worried again.

49

Sometimes, the Heart Overrules the Rules

One of the things we learned in "judge school," as new judges, commissioners, and referees, was that if you ran into some litigant who once appeared before you, you were never supposed to acknowledge that person due to confidentiality. Legal matters are private, and a hearty hello may cause embarrassment. For some reason, however, my Juvie litigants didn't seem to have that problem, and were loudly and openly happy to run into me. Except, of course, the ones who hated me forever and saw me as the Devil.

One time, I was on my way home from court. I was passing an outlet mall, and I stopped to do some shopping. On this particular day, I was walking through the mall when I heard someone yelling, "Hey!" I spun around to see who was doing the yelling when I saw four young women headed toward my direction. I recognized one of my teens in foster care, a lovely young woman who was doing well from what I remembered from court. She was in a good foster home, attending school, and allowed a day out with friends—a great sign. She ran up to me and gave me the biggest hug, all the while saying over and over to her friends, "This is my judge, this my judge." I smiled as she continued by introducing me to each of her friends. She then told her friends, "Hey! Say hi to my judge." Which they did. Moments like those warmed my heart. That girl put a big smile on my face for the rest of the day.

My next encounter was a little more unusual. I was headed into my synagogue for services when a car screeched into the parking lot. I turned to the car to find it contained one of my families. I had recently returned the children, and they were in the car with Mom and Dad. These parents had successfully completed their programs. I walked closer to the car to greet them.

Mom rolled down the window. "Hey Judge! We saw you pass us on the road, so we made a U-turn to follow you!"

I didn't know what to say.

"We just wanted you to see how well we were doing," the parents said. The mother then added, "Anyway, we just wanted to thank you for returning our children."

The parents, kids, and I were smiling as my Rabbi stepped up to all of us. He had heard what the mother said. We exchanged some pleasantries before I smiled and said my goodbyes as I then followed the Rabbi into the building. I was happy to see that family together doing so well and also, I figured that if my Rabbi heard my mitzvah (good deed), I would get a couple of extra points for wherever that would count!

Finally, in the you-can't-believe-this category, my last encounter. I was on a plane to Phoenix to speak at a conference there. My seatmate was a lovely African-American young lady named Lakesha. We smiled and started to chat.

"So, are you visiting Phoenix or returning home?" I asked.

Lakesha lived in Phoenix and was going home. We chatted for a bit before I asked her about her family.

Lakesha told me she was married. "We also have two small children, and my sister has been living with us for some years, but she's moving out because she has been accepted to nursing school."

My Juvie whiskers were twitching.

"I'm sorry, I don't mean to pry but...how did your sister come to live with you?" Lakesha took a beat before answering that their mother had died some years ago, and her father had started drinking. He had custody of their young child, but was increasingly physically abusive.

As Lakesha spoke, all of a sudden, a little flame started in the back of my mind.

I had to ask, "Did all of this happen in Phoenix?"

She shook her head no. "It happened in Los Angeles."

Lakesha then described how the Department had stepped in and removed her sister. Lakesha was then contacted and requested custody, which was granted after the proper investigation was done.

I just looked at her. Again, I had to ask, "Do you remember the name of your sister's judge?"

All of a sudden, Lakesha looked at me. Her eyes then got big.

"Oh my Lord, it's you!"

Lakesha had been to court once to get custody of her baby sister, who was now in nursing school. We both burst into tears. Then came the wettest hug I can remember. We held each other for the longest time.

I could have flown to Phoenix without the plane. And I would've never had that moment on the plane and other encounters like it if I abided by what I learned in "judge school."

What can I say? Sometimes, the heart overrules the rules...as long as no one gets hurt.

50

The Time I Brought My Grandson to Court

Daily, I heard cases, felt very close to the families, and thought they could tell that, good or bad, I was on their side for an outcome we could all live with.

I used humor but I never minced words as I liked to get to the heart of things and talk directly to the parents, and to all the children in the court. They and I have seen too much in life to dance around. I would check in with each child about his or her favorite school activities, classes, and extracurricular interests. I delivered very severe lectures on the consequences of domestic violence on children, and even passed out a simple article that explained it for the parents to read.

I used the carrot and I used the stick. I elicited laughs, I elicited tears. We were an active court. My goal was twofold always. Get these kids together, get them home, or get them to safety. My mantra was, "Better out than when they came in." I talked to the parents as if we were equals, I talked to the kids as if they were mine. I talked to aunts, uncles, grandparents, and made attendance at Al-Anon, is a program that helps families and friends of alcoholics recover from the effects of living with the problem drinking of a relative, or some program for enablers as a precondition for custody of the children during the reunification period. But one of the most unusual things I did was to take my three-year-old grandson with me to court.

My grandson lived in Northern California, and I valued every minute we could spend together. So, from the time he was about two-years-old, he went to court with me. He'd pull his little backpack on wheels behind him, filled with toys, movies, and snacks; he confidently negotiated the back halls where the bench officers were keyed in, and headed for my chambers. We set up the toys that I kept in my chambers, plus the DVD player, gave him a snack, and then we were off to court.

When the children filtered in, my grandson handed them their courtroom teddy bears. Otherwise, he played in and out of my chambers, the hall between the chambers and courtroom, and on my lap. I noticed something different happened when I had my grandson around. Everyone talked a little softer, smiled a little more, and kept their interactions with me respectful and polite. You would think that families who had either lost, or could lose, their children would be pretty angry about me having my grandson with me. They could have complained in writing, or to their attorneys, but no one ever did.

If I were removing children, my grandson stayed out of the courtroom, otherwise he was there. He became the mascot for our courtroom, with families asking about him when they were in court and he was not there. My grandson was a wonderful addition. Their inquiries spoke to the humanity of most of the families in court. Help them do it better, and they would. And my grandson humanized me, I think.

51

The Secret to Philly Cheesesteaks
and Successful Families

It is undisputed that the best cheesesteaks come from Philly. I grew up there and proudly make this claim. We also have the best hoagies. Some of us believe it is the bread. Philly water goes into the dough, which makes the dough just crispy enough to hold the ooey-gooey cheesesteak ingredients. Minute steak, that weird thin cut from who knows what part of the cow, is pounded into strips and charred on the grill. Next comes the grilled onions, then the piece de resistance, squeezed cheese from a can, plus personal additions.

It's a heart attack on a roll, and it's delicious!

Others have tried to replicate the sandwich; there are many restaurants here in California which claim to have "Real Philly Cheesesteaks!" They lie. They don't even come close. They are too clean, too pure, too healthy. And I know why they can't do it.

I believe the cheesesteaks made in Philly are made on grills that have never been clean. From day one, the grease is pushed to the back of the grill, when a new batch of steaks and onions goes on the grill. The grill is seasoned with fire, oil, grease, and sweat. Yum! Twenty years, thirty, fifty years of undefinable "schmutz." Nothing else tastes like a Philly cheesesteak.

So, I got to thinking. We are all seasoned in some way. Years of parental sweat, fire, and grease. The immigrant's journey, the work to get established in America, learning a new language, and trying to push your children to achieve, to push your children out of the sweat, to white collars, or white doctor's coats, professorial tweeds, or lawyers' sharkskin.

But in Juvie that was not what we saw. Kids were discouraged from getting past their origins and surroundings. Regardless of the parents' stated goals, kids who achieved did so in spite of their upbringings. Violence seemed to be the answer to every situation. Families continued the cycle, or spiraled down, generations of jail, drugs, or worse.

Why didn't it work for Juvie families? What happened that caused them to give up, or never buy into the American dream? What disconnect halted their upward climb to think that crime was more rewarding, that they felt entitled to beat their wives or children or both? To spend their money on drugs, not food? How had they been seasoned to believe they were worthless, or that their children were on their own?

Was the seasoning they got from individual ingredients, instead of that mix of ingredients, one ingredient helping the next to add to the flavor of the whole? Close-knit families, helping each other to rise, had always been our successful strategy. Fractured families, filled with failure, and lack of faith in each other, sent us angry and unhappy people.

If we did not have that fifty-year-old well-seasoned grill to work from, how did we make a great cheesesteak? We didn't. But we could try to create a different seasoning, one that fits the family we want to see. We start with the measure of understanding. We add some expectation of responsibility. A pinch of righteous indignation, just a pinch. And some tools to help make a new family recipe. And the new family can begin to season their own grill, and add their generations of sweat, fire, and elbow grease to those ingredients. They could proudly watch failure turn to success, and get their kids to excel and retire. And what a treat that would be for us all.

52

I Get to Be Silly... Foster Kids, Not So Much

So, I was visiting my relatives back east, staying with a close cousin, Buddy. We were having everyone over, and in my family, that was never less than thirty loud, hungry people. We were a rowdy bunch, with laughter as our currency, and everyone talking all at once.

We needed to go shopping to have food for our party. Buddy waited in the car, and I went into the market. With my cart, I started down an aisle, when I heard on the store's PA system Natalie and Nat King Cole's version of "When I Fall in Love." I love that song, and began singing along. Then I heard from the next aisle over, a man singing along with me. We slowly went parallel down our aisles and met at the end. Laughing, we finished the song together, and went into a warm hug. He was a lovely, older African-American man, who loved Nat as much as I did. We reminisced for a bit, then went our separate ways. Buddy wanted to know what took me so long, and when I told him he just rolled his eyes.

Why am I telling you this? Because I have been lucky and fearless enough to have lots of moments of joy like that. I have no problem making a fool of myself if the payoff is sunny.

In other words, I have had the luxury of stability, support, and encouragement.

Foster children live life on a tightrope. From the exaggerated fight or flight response, which impairs learning, brought on by their trauma, to the instability of life every day. "Who am I" is moot when your question is "Where will I sleep tonight? Where will I eat tonight?"

Family? Mostly gone. School? Don't make friends, for you may not be there tomorrow.

Clothing is rarely new, personal grooming in hair and body art is one way to express something. Their bodies are the only things they own. And, when things get really bad, sometimes even that is not true.

The lack of silly. The lack of joy. The healing powers of giggling, for boys and girls. We owe these children some of that. But the system only promises they will not be on the street. And if lucky, these kids will get foster parents with love in their heart as opposed to focusing on the paycheck in their wallets. We as a system need to create more opportunities for foster kids to play, to go on vacations, to express themselves in a silly way. We need to create opportunities for fun for them with no strings attached, just like many of us had growing up. This could include fishing trips, camping, going to the ballet, fun activities like sailing, roasting marshmallows, hiking, visiting theme parks, museums, getting their hair done, going to a fancy restaurant, and so on. I know the reality of bringing a lot of children in foster care together in large groups can cause havoc, so maybe smaller groups or pair siblings with a trusted adult, do more 1:3 trips to a baseball game, something, anything to add joy to these kids' lives.

If you work with kids in foster care and you don't have any ideas on what to do, then simply ask the child: "Hey, what would you like to do on a weekend someday? Something special just for you?" Don't wait until it's a child's birthday to make an extra attempt to show that you care.

Just a thought.

53

Juvie Really Is the Best Reality Show Ever

So, I have a little secret. I have a very dark sense of humor. And working in Juvie is like an idiosyncratic dream. The number of general screwups was just amazing. There were mainly very sweet people who were bound to be stabbed by every fork in the road. For both kids and their parents, the excuses for not getting things done were limitless. Whatever they needed was stolen, or left on a bus, or in a friend's car, but they couldn't remember the friend's name. "The dog ate my homework" was a life maxim. The bus didn't run on the day they needed to take a test. The friend who was to drive them to a visit got the flu.

I had a client whose children were removed because he had all three of them begging on street corners, and then used the money to buy drugs. He missed several drug tests, and when I asked him why, he had an answer.

"Uh, I was busy."

I tried not to roll my eyes when I asked him, "Busy at what?"

"Hmm," he said, "I don't remember."

I smiled. "Were you busy because you had been invited to the White House for lunch?"

This client shook his head, as if my question was serious. "Oh no, it wasn't because of that."

"Well," I said, "I'm thinking that would have been the only excuse I'd accept."

The man nodded. "I understand. I'll make sure I get tested."

In this case, he did and his children were returned to him, never in the system again.

There was another client who would have made a great appearance on a reality program. It was a mother who came to court on trial day wearing footie pajamas. They had bunnies on them, and were actually very cute. She wore boots on her feet, to go over the footie part. She testified very well. It didn't help.

Then there was the woman who sauntered into the courtroom wearing just a bra-style bathing suit top. Shirley was there to see if she was getting her kids back.

I had to set this mother straight. "Ma'am, you are going to have to leave the courtroom and cover up...also, you are not really being a good role model for your girls."

She left the courtroom in a huff and then returned wearing a blouse over the bra. Of course, it was wide open, no buttons.

"You know," I said, "buttons might be a good idea."

It was as if I was talking to a brick wall. A brick wall with an exposed bra.

I had one mother who slept through every hearing. Every one of them.

Then there was the father and his father who both had children with the same woman. Neither one had a problem with it either. In fact, they all lived together in one house as a happy family.

And who could forget the woman who had children by two brothers. But there were three brothers and she couldn't remember which two she had slept with. The brothers, however, did remember. She slept with them all.

One of my favorite fathers came in through the jail door. He seemed surprised he had been arrested, indicating that he took great steps to avoid it.

I was confused. "What do you mean by that?"

"Oh, I changed my name."

I looked at my paperwork. "Is Richard Jones not your real name?"

"Nope," he said, almost proudly. "My real name was 'Robert Jones.'"

I looked at him, stunned. "Why didn't you change your last name?"

He said, with all logic, "Because I wouldn't get my mail."

Then there were the kids who would tell you everything and then some, no matter what the issue was. They'd tell you that Dad spent the night last night when there was a restraining order. They'd tell where the drugs were hidden in the house. Whose boyfriend snuck in when the family was asleep. They overshared and spared no details.

Finally, there was nothing like Juvie extended families. The Jets and the Sharks are friendly rivals. When you had less than wonderful parents, they had parents who were awful or worse. And it was never, ever the fault of the specific side. It was always the fault of their kid, not our kid. And remember, in Juvie, we did not have only two sides. There were mothers and fathers galore, step-parents galore, twenty-nine million grandparents, innumerable aunts and uncles of all ages, and assorted others. We never actually got who some of the others were.

And everyone wants to talk. And talk. And maybe yell a little.

Total chaos. Total crackup. And I solved some of the problem by using a three-minute egg-timer that I had prominently displayed on my bench. Yes, I did. Believe it or not, no one has ever gone over the time limit. They stopped mid-rant. And we would relax a minute before the next person stepped up with a "You wouldn't believe me if I told you" moment.

I'm telling you: Juvie. The best reality show ever!

54

Friendships are Important,
but a Lifeline for Juvie Kids

I attended a memorial service for a friend who was on the bench with our group. She had passed away from a recurrence of cancer. It was a beautiful service at her daughter's home. Many of her longtime friends had lovely things to say, and anecdotes to share. Of course, I thought about my own friends, and family, and what I would have to say about them, or them about me.

I recalled a recent conversation with my grandson. He wanted to know if I had a "funny sidekick" when I was in school. He was starting the fourth grade, and was hoping his sidekick would be in his class again. I was really excited to tell him that not only did I have sidekicks, but he knew them! Each year for the Fourth of July, we went to Napa with the same friends from my childhood. My daughter's family joined us, so my grandson saw Barbara and Elliot every year since he was a baby. What a blessing, I thought, and thought also about the wonderful friendships I had, some over sixty years, some more recent, all treasured.

How lucky I was.

One of the other attendees at the funeral, a woman colleague I had known for years, mused aloud how she had not really understood how important friendships were. I knew she was a very private person, and I was not surprised at this confession of isolation. I knew, however, that she had a very loving and close family.

Why this musing? Because, as always, I thought about the children in Juvie. In dependency, trauma and abuse was the usual. We all do what we can to alleviate the physical symptoms, but as we know, the emotional toll is the more overwhelming and lasting. I think of children locked in home situations where they are unable to have a friend, for fear of discovery of family secrets. How completely isolated they are, and how serious this burden is.

We get lucky, though. Some kids make a friend, and then finally feel able to tell that friend, or the friend's parent, who then protects that child by informing the authorities. Or a teacher or counsellor is able to establish a rapport to make the child feel safe enough to tell what's really going on in the home. Finally, a trusted or beloved family member feels strong enough to buck the family dynamic and contacts some authorities. A petition is filed, and we all get to the task of healing the child and family. But what happens next?

The family is split up. The children are placed in different homes, unless a family member can take them all. They may be in vastly different places all over Los Angeles and its environs. Schools are changed, familiar neighborhood haunts are gone, classes are gone, classmates are gone. There were problems with transportation or phone privileges because the Foster Care Bill of Rights was not followed. We do our best to make the most of this new situation for the kids. I order sibling visits once a week, phone contact for the older children with parents and each other, and regular visitation for parents and family members who request it, but the visits are monitored, so no further trauma or inappropriate discussions can occur. The visits may be in a Department visitation room, to make sure the parent does not kidnap the children, or in a public setting. The visitation room is sterile and the visits are timed. There is no stability, no continuity. No birthday parties with friends from year to year, or regular holiday celebrations. I try to provide the children with activities besides school which interest them, but cannot always find something to fit into their packed afterschool schedules with therapy, visitations, and a foster parent's schedule.

Friendships in juvie are important as a lifeline to normalcy. When families fail, friends can be the saving grace. We should be maintaining friend contact as well as sibling contact, as part of our promise to our kids.

These children have experienced enough upheaval in their lives. Keeping friendships, besides the warmth and support provided, may also lead to permanent homes. I have had teachers, coaches, and best friends, provide new and rich lives for the kids the system took away.

55

It Just Takes One Person to Make a Difference

"Poverty of love and attention is the
most destructive poverty of all."
—Ursula K. Le Guin

Sometimes important lessons come at such unimportant times. At least that is how it feels.

My husband, Craig, and I were skiing with friends. I was new on the bench during this time. My friend Sandy and I were on a different slope, skiing together. I entered a three-person chair with Sandy at one end, me in the middle, and a young man at the other end. Sandy was telling me about teaching her new puppy how to behave. She was mentioning how she gives her puppy a small swat on the behind, when the young man turned to us.

"Are you talking about your child?" the young man asked.

We both turned to him at the same time and said firmly, "No."

"I was talking about my puppy," Sandy said.

Sandy and I laughed, but the young man did not.

"I...I have a child and I, uh, need some tips to be a good dad."

He seemed nervous, and we were both touched at the question.

I said to him, "Well, whatever you do, don't prop your baby up with the bottle on a towel. When you feed your child, hold him close, and look him in the face, so he can smell you, and hear you, and see you. It is called attachment and it is the single most important thing you can do for yourself and him."

The young man appeared to take in what I said. I wondered why he felt he needed to talk to strangers about this, but by this time we were approaching the exit. Sandy went to the right, I went up the middle, and he went to the left. As he started down the mountain, he turned to me and said, "I think I was propped."

His words have haunted me to this day, and informed many of my decisions and advice from the bench.

56

Henry

The most difficult part of my job was to try to find homes for our older kids. They moved from relative to relative, and home to home. As they continued to test limits and continued to be rejected, they escalated behavior and fell farther and farther behind in school. The very definition of a vicious cycle. Like Henry. He was ten when he came to me, for the usual reasons. He had exhausted a variety of relatives by fifteen, and was living in a group home when his case entered my court. I was a sucker for these kids, emphasizing and understanding their fear, anger, and sadness as a part of their behavior. I loved them all and was protective, as well as aggressive in pushing for as normal a life as we could manage. As a result, I was willing to host any number of relatives who would come forward, no matter how sketchy the background, if I was sure they were now appropriate. So, one day, Henry's grandfather appeared. He had a criminal history from many years ago and had been told he could not have Henry live with him. But I looked at this man, thin, with dark mahogany skin, razor sharp cheekbones, and a defiant aura to match. He dared me to say no, but he had little to say in his behalf. I then made a decision and said yes, and asked the Department to waive the prior history. They did, and Henry went to live with this man, his grandfather, whom he hardly knew.

At the six-month review, Henry was acting out, skipping school, and staying out all night. I thought we were through, and braced for the request for removal. I had my usual talk with Henry, and was the only one who displayed any emotion. Henry didn't look at me, the grandfather didn't look at me. But once the hearing was over, Henry's grandfather never said a word about having Henry removed. My heart was in my throat as I finished the hearing and set another six-month-date.

At the twelve-month review, Henry was following the house rules, going to school, and catching up. His grades were good, not great, but going up. His grandfather had him in afterschool activities, and Henry was smiling at me, and talkative. Grandfather never smiled or said a word.

This upswing in Henry's life continued for the next two years. Henry graduated on time, and with excellent grades. He was accepted to a good four-year-school for college and it came time for me to terminate jurisdiction over his case. Henry smiled at me when I congratulated him for his success. I was not only elated, I had a lump in my throat which was joy, as opposed to the fear of previous hearings. I looked at his grandfather, who sat stoically, as usual, before me. This time, however, his shoulders were a little higher, his face a little prouder. After this observation, I faced Henry.

"I want you to look at your grandfather today. I want you to remember that look of pride, and to never let that look leave his face as you go forward."

Henry promised, and I terminated his case with a hug. Grandfather never said a word.

57

If You Notice, Good Kids Tend to Self-Sabotage

A child who is violated by any person, particularly a person of trust, may look at the world as unsafe and view themselves as undeserving of good things in life, leading to self-sabotage.

Self-sabotage. A word that goes against everything we have been taught, and against common sense of our best interests. But this is exactly the behavior that bedevils so many of my kids. We know it even when we don't identify it by name. We see a person with a poverty-stricken childhood make good by hard work and talent. Then comes the DUI or the drug bust. The first of many stints in rehab. A slow fall from grace. Then nothing or, worse, a premature death by his or her own hand.

Now, with famous people, sometimes it is simply hubris; the sense that they are smarter than the rest of us and can do no wrong. That they will be excused or forgiven any transgressions due to their inherent "specialness." And sometimes very gifted people have a problem with addictive behavior in the same manner as the rest of us.

In a dependency situation there are several parallel timelines that are working at the same time. We are asking the Department to provide reunification services to the family; we are asking the family to take advantage of the services we are providing, so as to ameliorate the reasons the children were removed; and we are also providing a life for the children.

The life is one we hope will raise the child out of past and current life circumstances to make room for a better future. We provide education, and therapy, and try to keep the child attached whenever possible to family and friends. We check in regularly, and ask about interests outside of school. We try to connect the children and young adults with hobbies and first jobs. And always, we ask, "What can we do to help? What will make your life better?" And I ask them to make their own timeline, not ours, with a goal, and steps to get to the goal.

All of this is with a backdrop of a life already lived. These kids have not only not been raised in a vacuum, but they have seen and experienced more life than any of us, on either side of the bench. So we are part of the problem, under their suspicion and not seen as helpful.

How can we talk about the importance of education where there is no desk, no table, no lamp, no private place to do homework or study? Where generation after generation have never graduated from anywhere, and extended family are all "guests of the state." Where many families live cheek by jowl, with petty crime a way of life, and not only condoned, but completely acceptable?

Now, picture a child who, in spite of all the above, manages to get good grades, and aspire to better. A child who lives in a foster home, or with a relative who supports and encourages excellence, and a child who, in fact, is excellent. We are getting great report cards. We are getting social workers who are doing their jobs, and working to find colleges which will suit this child, including financial support. With huge amounts of gratitude and elation, off she goes to a new life.

All is well until we hear that good kid crashed and burned within the first year or two. Why? What went wrong? We did everything we could think of to do. But remember the traumatized child within the young person we sent away so easily. Remember that in order to succeed, this person will have to turn her back on her family, her friends, her neighborhood, her past, her childhood. And even when the family of origin mouths the words of support, they are tacitly reminding the child that getting "uppity" was unacceptable. That she should remember where she came from, and that moving up will be a lonely and foreign experience. "Don't go past your raisin'." In fact, while all of life is at the bottom of her barrel, there is no one waiting at the top. That decision is up to her, an ill-equipped, frightened child.

We have several top-notch organizations that try to fill that void. To offer mentorship and advice. We try to remember that while most college students can go home for summers and holidays, our kids will be homeless if they have to leave the dorms. So we argue to keep the dorms open for them.

And still the pullback is like a strong undertow at the beach. It takes a strong and determined swimmer to not go under but to stay afloat and get to the beach. We are getting better at looking at the past, and checking for the present so that our foster kids believe they deserve to prosper, deserve to succeed, deserve to keep rising. And to make sure the Self they have become does not need to be sabotaged because failure is familiar. They deserve to be celebrated. And loved.

58

Great Days in Court Do Exist

Oh, happy day! Adoption Day! Several times every year juvenile court closes to regular business in the afternoon, and does nothing but finalize adoptions all over the building. On Adoption Day, there will be balloons in the halls, and lots of fluffy teddy bears on the benches that usually are covered with files and Kleenex. The tissues are still there, but for the opposite of the usual reasons.

Because I was lucky enough to sit on the bench in California, I presided over every kind of adoption there could be. There was no limit on the definition of an adoptive family, on the color of skin, ethnicity, religious belief, gender classification. Hetero, homo, trans, you name it, so long as you were a decent person with love in your heart for unwanted children, you were a candidate. And so we celebrated.

On one particular Adoption Day, I finalized the adoption of twin boys who were taken in by two gay men. These boys required around-the-clock care to meet their special needs. The men took turns caring for them. The gay couple cried throughout their adoption proceeding, as did we all. They had gone through so much to get to where they were, and we were all so proud of this beautiful family.

Also on that day, there were five grandparent adoptions, which were always bittersweet. The children were protected, but at the cost of choosing them over the parents, those people the grandparents remember bringing into this world, and trying to raise them the best that they could. They were looking for a second chance to do it right. We hoped the same thing. There were two adoptions by aunts and uncles, one set from the mother's side, one set from the father's. They had taken these children into their homes, added on the expense of two children to the expenses of raising their natural-born children. There was a grace to these people, a worldview that did not count dollars and cents, just what was right.

These days were not like regular hearings, where relatives and friends may attend, but must sit in the back of the court. On Adoption Day, they could sit anywhere in the room, as long as the adoptive family was not impeded from hearing me. In the relatives and friends would come, with balloons and beautifully dressed children. Infants were in festive outfits, and we kept our fingers crossed that they would make it through without crying. If they cried, I just talked louder! Some families were small, some huge, some quiet as if in a religious ceremony, some raucous and cheering as they came into the courtroom.

Pictures were taken during the ceremony, and I posed with the new family after the ceremony. I always asked the older children to use my gavel, and at the count of three say, "Order in the court!" Merriment was the order of the day.

The merriment tone changed when a woman, alone, entered the courtroom with a seven-year-old child. Just the two of them, very unusual that they didn't have friends and family in tow. She was a doctor, divorced, and the boy was a foster child. She sobbed uncontrollably. Her soon-to-be adopted son tried to comfort her, not really understanding the tears. She tried to explain before finally getting herself under control. She believed she would never raise a child. Or have the happiness of being a parent. This traumatized child had thrived and could now turn and comfort her. The doctor now had a family. She couldn't believe her luck. I was thrilled for her.

A newly married couple, two women, had come to adopt the fourth child of the same drug-addicted mother. They just kept taking them one at a time. The older three children were excited and were told they each had had the same wonderful special adoption day.

I was honored to finalize the adoption for two of my friends' new grandchildren. Saints all. While there may be some sorrow and failures down the road, almost all these kids will not ever be back into this court again! This was exactly what we want. A great day.

59

Sometimes You Just Have to Laugh

To be part of juvenile court is to enter into a worldview slightly to the right of weird and to the left of insane. To put it mildly, it is skewed. In my day, we examined and argued the merits of "hard" versus "soft" molest. We articulated, with vehemence, that abuse was not abuse, but appropriate discipline, and that the drugs didn't hurt children if they didn't see them. That intent, when hitting your children, was relevant, and that parenting comes in many forms. That there were limits to the allowable government intrusion into the right to parent.

The result of this constant reinventing of acceptable boundaries was a mental outlook closer to Post Traumatic Stress Disorder (PTSD). The secondary result was a humor that was alternately mordant, macabre, or just plain bizarre. We joked about the unfunny. We joked about the just plain nuts, we joked about whatever it took to stay somewhat sane while trying to balance the rights of children with the rights of parents, and to actually help families in crisis. We never joked in public.

No way!

The other, albeit unconscious source of humor came inadvertently from lawyers, social workers, parents, relatives, either in words or in written form by way of letters or social study reports. These mistakes were sometimes poignant, but mostly hilarious. Combining an overworked social worker whose primary language was not English, with time crunches could be interesting. Add angry parents with no filter and we get some lightening of the load even for a minute. So, here are some of my favorites from thirty years of dedicated service to the unthinkable.

Blatantly inappropriate judicial opinions. Mine. Here are some of my doozies:

"Anyone who comes to court wearing a cross in the original size, did it."

"The size of the Bible matters."

"Originally stated dead fathers who show up at final hearings to challenge termination of parental rights are classified as miracles."

And the following mistakes are all from social workers' reports.

"Father is deceased. His address is Deceased, California. No services will be offered to him to regain custody of his children."

"The maternal grandmother is being looked at for placement of the children. However, at a meeting at the Department of Children and Family Services office, when her ex-husband showed up with his new wife, grandma tried to run them over with her car in the court parking lot. We think she may have poor impulse control."

"The parent exhibits potential versatile dangerous behavior."

"Matthew plans to be a professional football."

"Susie has constipation and has been referred to a dentist."

"Steven exposed his genitals and was sexually acting out. He received a library card."

"Mary is in her fourth foster home due to her behaviors. She called her teacher a bitch, chewed gum in class, asked a male student to bring a condom to school so they could have sex, but aside from that, foster mother says Mary has been very well behaved."

"Mother has a history of killing herself in 1994. She said she would rather have her daughter do things in front of her than do things on her behind."

"Mother is aware of her positive toxicology screen for herself and her new baby. She denies using drugs. She denies a drug history. Mother appears to be in denial."

"Social worker asked the mother to move away from the father. She said she did. Social worker notes that mother moved into the apartment immediately next door to the father. She asked the mother if she really thought the father could not find her there. Mother said she hasn't seen him in two days, so far, so good."

"Lucie has a good appetite and enjoys the other men in her home."

"Brandon exhibits some very immature behavior (note: Brandon is six-years-old).

"This family has violent alterations."

"The family home has guns, drugs, porn and cat odor."

"Father had gentile warts on his gentile parts."

Another father had an excuse for hitting his child, as the social worker states, "The father kicked the crack" out of him.

"The social worker apologized, in that she couldn't find the father, she was unable to service him."

In this apparently kinky family, the social worker noted that the "minor mother allowed her boyfriend to reside in her mother."

Add to this, a woman who pulled her rival's shirt off in a supermarket while her kids were there, social media gaffes kept forever to parade in court, paramours who were not allowed to have contact meeting at the Snooty Fox motel, and the Rooster Inn, with family finding out and mayhem ensued.

We love what we do and as inappropriate as it is to laugh at all this, sometimes, we just can't help it. It's a way to release steam, stress. Also, I mean, the things we see...you just can't make this stuff up!

60

The Business of Poverty Is Booming

The business of poverty is booming. Go to any seminar and what will you see? You will see well-dressed people present on serving people who wear clothes from thrift stores.

You see, there are so many needs, and a lot of Federal and State dollars to be gotten. Follow the money.

It is easy to be cynical about the well-paid heads of "poor people" agencies. They come to conventions, set up booths, give out pens and tablets, as they extol their programs. They provide residential facilities for special needs children, drug treatment programs for addicted parents and children, parenting programs, psychological counseling, hospitalization for those with mental health issues, housing consortiums, and a plethora of adjunct services to help lift up a poverty-stricken and dysfunctional family after the cycle of poverty and dysfunction.

They also mushroom according to the flavor of the month issue, then fade and disappear when the media fades, or the money runs out, and there is a new kid in town.

"Try this if your kids are out of control!"

"Try this if your loved one has relapsed."

"This therapy is what works!"

"We have the answers."

Slick and rehearsed, they all look great.

Until they are not. Until the group home is found to be almost a storefront, and the residential parents looking after the eight or ten juveniles are almost as young as the kids they are watching. Therapy is sporadic, and therapists are jaded and tired, or brand new and accumulating the hours necessary for a license. They need to be supervised. Sometimes they are.

I go to these seminars, and conferences, and institutes, and I listen. I get excited, along with everyone else committed to these families. We have breakthroughs, and I am eager to try them out. My friend says that when we leave these conferences, I am like Tigger, jumping up and down to try something new, and she is like Eeyore, bent over by the amount of new work we will have. It cracks me up, the metaphors are so on target.

Then we try out the new theories. We try out the new paradigms. We try out the new therapies. Cognitive therapy instead of deep analysis. Domestic violence is not handled by a good talking to, but by arrests, or restraining orders. Shelters spring up and provide classes in much more than just staying safe.

And sometimes the new works. Sometimes the new really is better. We see families bloom, and prosper. Kids are returned faster and stay home. Families I see regularly do not come back.

The line workers, the dedicated on the ground workers, who are underpaid and overworked, bear no resemblance to the suits we listened to. The good programs hire good people, the bad money-grubbing programs are only found out later, after their large Federal grants go missing, and large homes and cars are bought. There are way too few State auditors who check in on all the homes, and no auditors checking on the programs. We do not know until it is too late, the damage is done, the program packed up and gone.

The business of poverty is booming. Wouldn't it be cheaper and more reasonable to provide families with decent housing, good and safe schools, child care that enriches the child, and a community that values all its neighbors?

The suits don't think so.

And yet we listen to the people who financially benefit from the problem and not the people on the ground. We are the family helpers.

61

What Makes a Father?

Laura weighed all of about eighty pounds soaking wet. She had three kids by three different fathers. Two of them were in court, each asking for custody of their respective children.

That was an interesting and unusual case because normally, we didn't see fathers showing up. If they did, it was because they mostly wanted out, not in. In addition, these fathers were both working, and respected members of the community. They had no criminal history.

I wished I didn't come across as cynical, but facts are facts. Most of the time, fathers do not show up like they did in Laura's case. I wished that wasn't the case, but it was and still is now. I wanted the opposite. I wanted all dads to step up, to be prepared to be role models for their children. I wished they didn't beat the mothers of their children, or use their women's money to buy drugs, or alcohol.

Fathers are a lynchpin of our system. Have a good one, and you can turn the case around. Have a bad, absent, or unknown one, and it is Tuesday. We spend time carefully figuring out what kind of fathers we have. Alleged by the mother, and gone. Legal by a DNA test, and gone. There is no consequence for deserting your kids and never coming back to court with Juvie. Then they move on and don't provide a further address. Or, a presumed father, one who is either married to the mother or has held himself out as the father of the child, and had the child in his home. We don't mean that he lives in the house of the mother's mother, or his mother, or any apartment the welfare check pays for, or the mother pays for with her one to three jobs. We mean he has a home, and supports that home with actual money. Sound simple? Think again, it rarely happens. Add in the fact that lying and actual confusion as to the identity of the father is common. You are shaking your head now. Don't bother. We in the child welfare system have heard it all.

But to my surprise, and delight, that was not what we had. We had two decent fathers in that courtroom that day. Two men ready and willing and able to step up for their kids. I was all ready to place the kids with them when the eighty-pounder alleged druggie, with an anger management problem, erupted. She jumped up, screaming that each of the fathers did drugs with her. That they both beat her. That they never saw their children.

"I lied about them being good fathers!" she said, screaming.

In response to this outburst, I ordered the kids to be removed from the court, all the while thinking, "Oh no!"

This lady will never give up. She will hound these guys until her kids grow up, and beyond. Based on experience with these types, I already know that she will begin making false allegations the minute they leave court. So, what was I to do? The law says if there is a parent able to care for the child, and there is no risk posed by that parent, we must close the case with a family law order.

These kids were going to be examined, questioned, re-examined, and hounded by social workers constantly. The family court had no choice but to follow up when the calls and allegations were made. But if the case stayed in Juvie, the judge would know her, know her patterns, and tell the department to leave the children alone.

I decided to overrule the mother's objections and place the kids with their respective fathers. The kids would be raised in three homes, one to each father, and the fatherless one would be in foster care. I wanted to make sure the siblings saw each other, so I ordered that in Juvie, and made sure that happened.

I explained to the fathers what I was doing and why. In response, the fathers calmly accepted the order, but the mother yelled and screamed.

As much of a headache as Laura was—to the court, to the fathers, and, no doubt, children—thankfully, those fathers took their children in and raised them. I never saw them again.

62

What to Do with Mothers
Struggling to Care for Themselves?

I have been musing on the latest cutbacks in access to health care for women and teens. New and safer methods of contraception, and the ability to provide abortion in a secure, legal setting, are in danger more than ever. It is so very disappointing and frustrating, especially since our numbers of foster children continue to rise. Many people in poverty have no way to access easy contraception. Many of them don't even know they are pregnant until it's too late.

One particular case reminds me of this issue of limiting contraceptive care. Her name was Ana. She was fifteen-years-old. She came into court with her head down. She had a furrowed brow and a quizzical look on her face. She was short, skinny, and seemingly much younger than her fifteen years on this earth. Her lawyer intimated to me that she would need a "guardian ad litem" for the case. This means that she would be unable to assist her attorney with her case, in that she did not understand why she was in court. Guardian ad litem stands in the shoes of the client, and makes the decisions in consultation with the appointed or retained counsel. Even if the client is right there in court.

To determine that drastic step, the client is entitled to a mini-hearing of sorts. The court inquires, and then makes the decision. It is a step below a conservator, which is permanent.

In this case, I asked Ana if she knew why she was in court. She said she didn't know.

"Ana, I am going to ask you a few questions. Will that be okay?"
Ana nodded.

"Do you know if you had a baby?"
Ana said she wasn't sure. "I think so?"

"Ana, what day of the week is it?"
She looked to her lawyer, then me. "Tuesday."
It wasn't Tuesday.

"Who is the President of the United States?"
Ana again looked at her lawyer. "Um, I don't know."

I asked Ana more questions but she could not answer any of them. There are two types of people who cannot answer basic questions, the mentally ill and the developmentally disabled or challenged. Because Ana fit into the latter category, I appointed a guardian ad litem for her. Doing this would be a very difficult issue for the lawyer in dependency, as it tainted the possibility of adequate parenting. Whereas a mental illness or challenge is a mitigating factor in criminal law, it is the opposite here.

Back to Ana, a developmentally disabled mother. Her lawyer argued that the baby belonged with her. Ana herself was in the system, and her foster mother was happy to have both her and the baby there. So I allowed this placement while understanding that in reality, the foster mother would be raising the baby instead of Ana. What would happen when Ana turned eighteen and had to leave the foster home? Or chose to, and takes off with the baby? I was not allowed to speculate on that, even though I did, because that was not the current situation. I was only to deal with risk t that time. I could look at prior behavior to decide future detriment, but in that case, she and her baby had been well taken care of in the foster care system, so there was no evidence that the baby was at risk.

Let's get real here. Did I think Ana should have had a baby? No. Did I think Ana should keep her baby? No. Did I get to say that? No.

Keep your fingers crossed.

This was a problem I faced whenever I faced the serious problem of a mentally disabled person having a child. My head said one thing, my heart pretty much agreed with my head on that one, but the law saw it differently. There was no law that precluded a mentally incompetent person from having a baby. Nor should there be. We have had our period of eugenics in the United States, and that mindset is as close to fascism as our country went. Yet, giving birth when one didn't even understand how it happened, what to do about it, or even that a birth occurred, was frustrating and heartbreaking for all. Especially the mother, who had no way of parenting without twenty-four-hour assistance.

So, what do we do with people like Ana? What do we do with our eleven-year-old mothers, our mentally ill homeless women who get raped and have babies as a result? We try to get help from family, from community resources, from wherever we can try to teach, model, and be hands on. We know that other parents with disabilities can parent. Blind, hearing-impaired, and parents who cannot speak all can, and have, parent successfully. But they have their faculties intact, and new technologies to help.

The bottom line is that most of these parents do not get to keep their children. It makes sense, but it also feels awful.

63

My Promises to Kid Runaways

Destiny was back. I was delighted but not optimistic. Destiny had been back before. Many times. And within weeks of placement, she would run again. We would issue a warrant, she would be brought back and returned to foster care.

Chris was back. I was delighted but not optimistic.

Destiny and Chris were two of many runners I had in my court. From age fourteen up, these kids would take off at the slightest excuse. I was at my wits' end. What could I do to keep these kids around long enough to help? To help physically? To help emotionally? To help them choose a path out of poverty and foster care?

"My kids," as you might imagine, come from poverty. From poverty to welfare poverty, to deep homeless poverty. They also have a poverty of love, support, affection. Not all, however. Many of our families do everything they can to fix the circumstances that brought them to Juvie, and regain custody of much-loved children. But too many were "throwaway kids," wanted by no one. Trust me, not even you would want to take in some of these kids.

And, by the way, they don't trust you either.

So out they go, to the streets, to live with begging, filth, fear, and loneliness. And here they come. The sex traffickers, luring our high-risk kids with false promises of both tangible and intangible betterment. Oh, how talented they were at seduction. It was their trade, and they plied it with panache and patience.

The sex traffickers were the anti-system.

The reality of trafficking for these kids was no different from the life they left. No different from how they were treated there, both boys and girls telling me they were now getting paid for what was taken from them before. Add addiction and isolation, the psychology of people doing what they knew, chaos feeling normalized, it is no wonder why these kids remained lost. Lost eventually to the adult criminal system, until, at some point, enlightened people realize these kids were victims, not criminals, and laws were finally passed that precluded them from being arrested when found. So, here they are again. In my court. And ready to flee. What to do?

Here was Chris on Monday. Here was Destiny on Tuesday. Tamika on Wednesday. Lucia on Thursday. I raised my right hand. I asked the kid to do the same. Some complied. Some didn't. Let's take Chris.

I said to Chris, "I do not promise what I cannot deliver. I promise to help you find your path in your way, by your rules, as much as I can, if you promise not to run for one week."

Chris, with his hand raised, promised.

I asked him what he wanted for that week?

"Can you help me try to find my uncle?"

I said I would and set his hearing for one week. In that week, Chris had not run, and had attended school. We found his uncle, and Chris had had some limited contact with him. The uncle was simply not going to be a resource for Chris. But we set another hearing in one more week. Next week, Chris was still in his foster home, and at school. Huzzah! Chris and I discussed school, added some activities, and I set another hearing for another week, then a full month. After that month, I told Chris I didn't need to see him for another month. He smiled and agreed. After another month, I told him three months. He beamed and nodded. Then we went for six-month regular hearings, until he was ready for college. Chris stayed with me for two more years and went to a two-year school. Then he exited out of Juvie, and entered the military. And out of my life. That was always a good thing. I think my kids who didn't come back with their own kids, other than a visit, were exactly where they needed to be.

I have used the "promise" method for all my runners. Some promise back, some won't or don't. I felt they needed someone to push the system to actually work. No falling through the cracks for these kids. I don't have all success stories, by any means. Trust, both ways, was the currency of Juvie. And trust comes with time, with patience, with the right kind of seduction. Watch out, traffickers, we are learning your ways. And we can offer better options than your shiny things. We offer a future.

64

Lost in the System

A group of people walked into the courtroom and separated out into Mom's position, Dad's position, and some relatives stayed in the back, including the maternal grandmother. For the most part, I usually can tell right away who is who. Not with this group, however. I had to wait and watch the parents come forward and take their seats.

You see, Mom was extremely skinny, pale, and shaky. Dad was healthy looking, heavyset, and young, young, young. It turned out, he was fifteen years younger than Mom and not only that, but Mom's oldest child was almost the same age as Dad!

Of course, Dad was not the father of her other children—all eight of them. Each with a different father, each in the system, each not returned to Mom, but in permanent homes. And here she was again. Clearly, still using. This baby, like all her other children, was born under the influence.

Dad, however, was still reeling over the birth of his first child. At twenty-four, he was dazed, scared, and could not have looked more out of place. I'm used to fifteen- and sixteen-year-old parents, with crossed arms and "whatever" attitudes, with their parents in the back prepared to do it yet again. But cases with hugely skewed ages of the mother and father had their own issues. Usually, it is a very young mother, and a much older father. We immediately suspect trafficking with the father as her pimp. Sometimes that is right, sometimes not.

It is not unusual in our society to accept an older man with a younger woman. We call her a trophy wife or partner. We see them in our court for all the usual reasons. We must look at the father as a possible custodial parent, unless we can prove coercion. With trafficked girls, they will not say rape. It is a very slippery slope. Even the laws barring a rapist from getting custody are not very old. As a lawyer, I had a case in the 1980s where the known rapist did short time, and got custody. I represented the mother, who continued to use drugs. Not surprising, since she was a rape victim. Also, not surprising back then that, because the rapist was able to get a job, housing, and child care, he got the baby.

While that cannot happen anymore, due to family code changes, we still look closely at the couples to decipher hidden clues to their relationship.

In this case, in court, I could see that that young man was in no position to parent. He had no job, or regular home. He wasn't sure what was going on. I was not really comfortable, to say the least, that this was a happy couple based on everything I had read and seen in court. I put the baby in foster care. My guess was we would not see that young man again. And the department had recommended no reunification services for the mother, due to the loss of her other children.

So, that baby will have no idea that his mother may be a professional, in the oldest sense of the word, and his father was a sad young man who thought he got lucky.

Now that the father is no longer a young man though, I wonder if he tried to get his baby back.

And this, folks, is how some kids get lost in the system. One can only hope that baby got adopted into a good home.

65

Foster Kids Need Quiet Time

When I was a child, from the time I can remember, each of my report cards said the same thing. The grades were fine, but the comment was, "Sherri talks too much in class." Every report card until "deportment" wasn't graded anymore. So, I think it surprises people to learn that I was basically a very shy person. To this day, I am very happy being alone. I treasure solitude, and have my whole entire life. As a child, I remember the long, long walk to the nearest library. Every Saturday, I walked alone, to take out the books I was allowed to take out. I must have been ten-years-old or so. As a teen, living in safer times, I could take a bus to the Jersey shore, two hours away, and walk on the winter boardwalk, watching the dark-blue ocean, just me and the whirling, screeching ocean birds. I had many friends, and a glorious, fun childhood and adolescence, but I really craved time alone to just be quiet. Because I was essentially in a safe world, I could carve out that time, then rejoin my "life in progress" at will. Time with friends, time with family, time for school, all without much angst, or even soul searching. The solitude I wanted was simply to turn off the underlying, never-ending acceptable teen behavior. I know that now, but didn't know it then. Psychologists talk about nature versus nurture, who we are, plus or minus how we are raised. I would add neighborhood, as peer pressure surely adds to who we become.

I think about foster kids. Their peer pressure is quite different from how mine was. I had to excel in school, and I had to stay properly chaste until marrying an acceptable professional, ideally just when I received my degree. I lived at home up to that marriage, which happened right on target.

Foster kids are not encouraged to excel in school. Most of the older kids are caring for their younger siblings to get them to school. They have no time for themselves, at home. School is not a value, books are not in the home, and sexual behavior is not even an issue from early adolescence.

I worry that foster kids get no time alone. I have friends who grew up with many siblings and had no room for alone time, and they loved it. But when you are in a situation fraught with daily conflict, drugs, abuse, how do you find time to just be quiet?

Quiet time just does not happen in foster care, or in a group home. Every hour has either chores, school, or therapy. Visitation by parents or sibling visits take up more time. There are no group friends, few movie dates, or mall days, long walks to a park, or picnics. These kids are in automatic survival mode 24/7. Every day is a new day filled with challenges. There is no time for restorative silence. And they need it more than most kids.

Everyone needs time to be alone.

Now I get to be quiet. I want the same for foster kids. A quiet moment to just be.

66

I See Children Not Be Children

So, there she was. The epitome of so many girls like her. In court, there was a young woman, between thirteen and eighteen-years-old. She was gorgeous, multi-ethnic. She had been removed from her mother. Dad was either unknown or out of the picture. If there was a dad, there was a strained relationship. With little contact. Or the dad had another primary family. Maybe there was a stepfather, or Mom's never-ending parade of boyfriends. The young, beautiful girl in my courtroom had had a revolving door of a life. She was in one home and out the door when Mom broke up with the latest boyfriend. She was in one door and out the other at school. She had no time to make permanent friends. But she was always popular with the boys; girls who look like her gets lots of attention from them.

Her shell was complete. No one could get in. Beautiful on the outside, dead on the inside. Tough on the outside but terrified inside.

Did she know that education was important? Yes, but that didn't matter in her world. Nothing mattered. She was isolated within an aura of sociability. The truth of her life was too painful to live, let alone share. She may have cut her skin, to deflect the internal pain. She dressed provocatively, or stylishly, or sloppily. Her makeup ranged from non-existent to full magazine cover.

Sometimes her mother showed up to court, sometimes her mother was happy to get rid of the competition. Too much attention from the boyfriends, after all. And sometimes too much attention turned into sexual abuse and violence. The girl would get blamed of course, as they usually did, by both the mother and the boyfriend.

What kind of people were these? What kind of people would raise a child to be abandoned and violated? People whose lives may have been exactly the same as the young girl's but who had not learned enough or cared enough to break the cycle.

And yet another beautiful, young girl was in front of me. Sitting before me as a bundle of perfect anger. Prickly doesn't begin to describe her. Buzzing with disinterest, more like. Bristling with fury, I could actually see her aura. It wasn't white. Her arms were crossed. Her body was there, but her mind was out of the room. It was back to whatever bastion of safety she had managed to put together.

I said, "I have a problem."

She looked elsewhere.

I said, "You are gorgeous."

She looked at me.

I said, "You are also smart."

She looked away but then back at me.

I said, "I know this because I have eyes, and I can tell you have managed to get this far and still be alive."

At this, I sometimes may get a faint smile, but if not, I at least have her attention.

I said, "Do you realize what prime meat you are?"

This truth gets a bit of outrage as no one wants to be called "meat."

We talked about trafficking, in the hopes that I was not too late. Our trafficked girls required a different response. We talked about her current circumstances. I asked her and girls like her if there was anyone in her entire family she might want to see. If there was anything in this world she would like to do? If she had any dreams for herself? I talked to her about pregnancy, and my hopes in that direction. But mostly I tried to ask questions that would elicit her talking. About anything. Anything that would help me crack that shell enough to reach inside, and help her start to dream. To aspire. To see a future. To start to envision it.

I must get the inside to match the outside. To get her to where she sees her beauty not just in the mirror, where it had not been an advantage, but in her mind, and in her heart, and in her possibilities.

She sat before me. A beautiful young woman. Alone. I must convince her I am on her side, and that I see her. I see her.

67

The Right Kind of Rebel

So, there I was, another day in court. I had four kids before me. This was a regular hearing date. The issue was the usual, were the kids to remain in foster care, or be returned to their parents? This was the crux of my work, repeated twenty to thirty times a day. It was easier when the kids were with relatives, but the basic structure remained the same. The oldest child, a teenager, was completely out of control. Her reaction to her situation was to rebel against everything and everyone in her life. She stayed out all night, stopped going to school, and fought everyone who tried to help.

I've seen it again and again. The children's frustrating knowledge that the people who were supposed to love and protect you, loved someone or something else more. Like the women who left their kids for man after man, shedding children as they went. Drugs, of course, more powerful than any emotional tie. There was alcohol, and plenty of it, permeating the family, including the kids themselves. Some of my kids started drinking at age eight or nine. Plentiful cheap booze was always around and it numbed the enormous pain until it caused more pain. More pain, more booze until finally, the family implodes. Jobs get lost for their final time, arguments turn into fights, fights turn physical, the police get called, and a petition is filed.

The parents of these four children had done little or nothing to regain custody.

A parenthetical to these cases has to do with time and motivation. The original motions of guilt at themselves and anger at the system give way to two action agendas. One was to start programs immediately, making a concerted and honest effort to turn these parents into the role models and nurturing parents that children expect. There were challenges along the way, some failures, some relapses even if the path was a resolute one. We supported these parents, adding more visits and fewer restrictions along with their successes. And, if it worked, the children would go back home. We applauded the different trek the parents had negotiated to regain custody, and happiness was felt by all in the courtroom.

The other response was to realize that with the kids gone, both responsibility and guilt went along with them. The parents would get to sleep in late, party hard, more drugs, more of whatever felt good in the moment; this had now become a lifestyle without parenting, and once that happened, getting back on track was increasingly difficult.

And the kids know. They know if they were valued or not. And as the parents' anger and embarrassment faded, the kids absorbed the emotional toll of those poor decisions. Anger, embarrassment, pain, and confusion, all played out in the courtroom for all to see.

And so the sibling set of four came to court that day, one case on my crowded calendar. The parents loudly complaining about the system, and declaring their love for their children. Having done absolutely nothing to prove it, which was excruciating for the kids.

So, to my teenage rebel. Why go to school? You are worthless. Why make friends? You are worthless, and don't know where you will be living tomorrow. I am actually surprised at the fact that she is not using drugs, or drinking, or pregnant. She is one of many of my kids who do not move on to self-destruct, reminding me of how smart, or at least street smart, these kids are, and how deserving they are of our good parenting. Because I am now shifting away from the parents, moving toward what I can do for my rebel. I have read the report prepared by the social worker, who has spoken to family members, including one of the grandmothers. Grandma has commented on how smart her teenage rebel granddaughter is, and how much she wants for her. How she must go back to school, and have a future.

I mentioned to my rebel what her grandmother has said. I then said, "Allow me to introduce myself. I am the voice of your grandmother."

The teenage rebel smiled, knowing I meant to use my authority to help her choose a wiser life course. A better one. Just like her grandmother wanted.

I am happy to say that in this case, that is what happened. The teen rebel returned to school and although she could have, she did not rebel in school. Instead, she rebelled against the low expectations of her given her background.

She rebelled against her parents by not becoming like them.

68

Some People Are Truly Evil

One of the worst parts of the job is dealing with people who are so evil that they cannot really be considered human anymore.

The people about whom I am speaking are rapists of newborns, men who rape girls knowing they are HIV positive, women who sell their children for economic reasons, or to keep a man, or to stay in the United States.

Usually these people are arrested, but it takes time, and sometimes they are not arrested but should be. With some of these people sitting right in front of me, I can only wonder why these women haven't dumped these men.

Allow me to give a more specific example of true evil.

I had a case with a girl named Lisa. Lisa was thirteen. Thirteen and pregnant. The father of the baby was her own biological father. She denied it. He denied it. Her mother denied it. There were four other girls in the family, three of them younger than Lisa, one older. The father was not in the household, but I know he was in touch with the mother. In fact, I know this because when he was arrested, before was bailed out, he called the house every day, and talked to Lisa's older sister so that she could talk Lisa out of stating he was the father. It worked.

We could not do a DNA test because we could not find him after he was bailed out, so we did a relative DNA search, and all relatives except the father were exempted.

Now, here they were. Lisa sat in court next to her mother; they were holding hands. The baby had been born, and due to the proximity of genes, had serious abnormalities. The baby had been determined to have a possible two-year life span, maybe less. Lisa, a baby herself, and the grandmother of the baby had taken classes to care for the child, and were apparently doing a good job. Lisa's lawyer, who was Lisa's lawyer both as a minor and as a mother, asked that I dismiss the petition which was filed on the new baby since the now fourteen-year-old was taking care of the baby, and there was no risk to that baby.

I looked at Lisa's lawyer. Not in this lifetime. I did not dismiss the petition.

Now as to the petition for Lisa, as to her own minority and risk. Piece of cake.

At some point, they will find this guy, and rearrest him. I know what he will say. He will say it was consensual between himself and his thirteen-year-old daughter. Yep, good one.

I really couldn't do much there. The baby would die, Lisa would stay with her mother. I shook my head. One more tragedy by an entitled, evil person.

Then I looked at the wife/mother/grandmother. The one in denial. The one protecting this man. I really looked at Lisa's mother and saw the devastation on her face. Her husband, the father of five children, the breadwinner, the dad. He sexually abused one of their daughters and there was nothing the mother felt she could do about it. She was stuck. That look on her face told me that she knew she was a horrible mother for not protecting her daughter, but what could she do?

I took a minute to get over my anger and disgust, and really see Lisa's mother. I had to say something.

I said, "I see you. I cannot fathom what you must be going through. You need support to see you through this. I see that now."

She nodded at me, sadly, and mouthed, "Thank you."

Some people are truly evil and some feel like they are truly helpless. Part of this job was to see the difference.

69

We All Need Soup for the Soul

So there I was the other night, watching *Top Chef* on the Bravo channel. I love that show and similar shows on the Cooking Channel as well. I was struck by the repeated references to mothers and grandmothers. As in, "I learned from her, and was taught by her, but my lasagna, chicken soup, mole just isn't as good as hers."

I started thinking about why this was so. I thought about my own closest grandmother, my father's mother, and her cooking. When I was in her kitchen and watched her cook, I noticed she never measured anything. A pinch of this, a pinch of that was the recipe. You had to feel it. And I realized that her food always included that pinch of love. Of warmth. Of pride. Of family. The recipe was, of course, never the same when I tried to make it, as an adult. It was good. It was fine. But it was not the same.

As for my mother's cooking? Terrible! I mean terrible. Just terrible. Really. Meat you could put under shoes if necessary, vegetables all the same color, brown, and limp. You know, terrible. Except her pizza. She made pizza from scratch every Friday night. Absolutely, they were the best pizzas ever. Go figure. She also made the family brisket, a recipe my daughter and I both use to this very day.

But our house was the central meeting place for all our friends, family, and neighbors. We always had more than four for dinner. My sister's friends, my friends, my parents' friends, whatever relatives from our huge family happened by, were all welcomed. Noise, laughter, yelling abounded. I don't think anyone actually ate the food. We did have some unmarried male cousins who stopped by suspiciously near dinner. Maybe they ate.

In addition, our house was the unofficial teen center. Our basement had been finished with knotty pine walls, a forty-five record player, and room to dance. There was always a bucket of Charles Chips potato chips, and pretzels on the table. To this day, when talking to my old friends from home, every one of them comments about old Charles.

On snowy days, when school was closed, our front lawn was the snow fort, a huge group of teens was baking cookies in the kitchen, and Friday sleepovers were the norm. Three or ten on the couch, beds, floor, it just didn't matter. There were games, and dancing in our knotty pine basement. It was a magical childhood in the three thousand dollar row house in Philly. Even adolescence was fun in the late 1950s.

Then came my family. I cooked healthy, well-balanced meals and we ate together. If it didn't have bread around it, my daughter wouldn't eat it. My son ate tuna fish for lunch every day for four years. My children's friends were welcomed anytime. And my kids marched in social justice protests with me from childhood, saw me active in community affairs and hold office in several community organizations, and they supported me as I went to law school at almost forty. My grandson had his first march at ten. His parents said he takes after me. Right on!

Where is this going? To nourishment. To what constitutes nourishment. It does not have anything to do with food. It has to do with whatever fills you up. Satisfies you. Gives you that cocoon of safety, to step out, take risks, grow up.

For our kids in foster care, unless the parents get it together, or someone loves them and keeps loving them no matter what, their cups will not "runneth over." There are no family traditions, funny or warm. They may have traditions not so funny. Sleepovers? Where? Friends for dinner? Not if you are moved every six months. They, as we, need to be part of something. Of a community. With some shared history. Without some nourishment of the soul, they wither, and give up.

We need to see these families as they are. And help them as they are. As a community. To serve our at-risk families a nice big bowl of hope.

70

Old Friends (Not that Kind of Old)

I was invited (ordered) by some dear friends to a birthday party in Atlantic City. It was a nostalgic venue, bringing with it weekends as a teenager. There were eleven of us, celebrating our seventy-fifth birthdays and the joy of having gone all through school together. I even brought along our junior high school graduation photograph. I was a little concerned, going all the way from California. While I was good friends with a few of the women, some of them I hadn't seen since high school graduation.

What would they be like?

What if we had nothing in common anymore?

But my friend Leslie said she made a hotel reservation for me, and I needed to just send her a check already! Oh, well. Here I go. Off to Philly, then shuttle to the hotel. Hot. Hot. Humid. Hot. When I checked in, I dropped my suitcase in my room, and headed for the room designated as our meeting room.

There, at the meeting room, I saw the group of eleven women and stood very still. It was like a time warp. I soon discovered that each and every one of those women were just as wonderful as I remembered them. Funny, warm, smart, they looked fabulous to boot! Some hips were not the original. Some knees were not the original. Two leaned on a cane, there were two widows, a few on second or even third marriages, most in the original! Two had lost adult children, an agony hard to imagine. We all chatted, hugged, and stayed close together that first day, sharing and oversharing the last sixty years, offering each other support, listening to pain, but mostly expressing tons of love. We also howled with laughter the entire trip! What an experience, I tell you. One I will never forget. Bless you, Leslie. You really know me.

And that is the point.

They remember me. I remember them. We share memories of the days when we were being formed. One of the women said how proud she was we were friends with her even though she was not in college-bound classes. Believe me when I tell you, it never occurred to us who was where. It was about personality, about ability to dance, and just about being kids together. It was about getting home from school in order to watch *Bandstand.* Not *American Bandstand.* Not yet. For us in Philly, it was a local dance show. There is something besides the memories that happened here. It is a "knowing." A recognition of who we were when we were changing the most.

We knew some of each other's parents, we slept over at each other's houses, and shared school lunches. Almost all the parents have passed away. We remembered them together. We remembered a friend also gone, and raised a glass to her memory. It was a deep and wonderful vacation to the past. And then to the present, and then to the future.

When I think about what my dependent children need, I always have emphasized family, education, growing up healthy and outside their circumstances. Volunteers, tutors, family visits, sibling contact, all are important to keep that sense of belonging somewhere. I never thought of the belonging to a line of friendships who knew you when, and after when. To gauge your future by knowing your past. What a loss. I felt such despair when I realized friendship was one more thing these kids had lost.

When will we learn how to really help these families? To heal them and stop the downward spiral. We can start by not only making sure they are connected to their families, but to their childhood friends as well, since we all need friends. Every one of us.

71

The Red Shoe

Let me tell you about the red shoe.

I have been blessed with a fairly good reputation for speaking, and have been invited to either lecture or take part in many dozens of symposia, conferences, high school classes, and college classes. They range from teaching at the State of California Judicial College, my most prestigious gig, to high school career day.

I have taught classes on the Indian Child Welfare Act, educating children in foster care, and participated in many panels on basic dependency, and other issues. I have been part of several documentaries, one on television and others as teaching tools.

My resume is replete with every kind of speaking engagement one can imagine. Students, other bench officers, community partners, I love them all.

But one of my favorites was an ongoing juvenile justice class at the Cal State University, Long Beach. The participants were young adults in the undergraduate school. They were all planning careers which spanned the panoply of careers associated with families. Social worker majors, probation, police, law, psychology, counseling, medicine; they all took this class as part of the required studies. I was asked to come and lecture on juvenile court, how it worked, and the list of players and their roles. I went over a short timeline of Juvie hearings, explaining what they were for, and passed out a sheet that explained the timeline and defined the process. Then I moved to participatory engagement with the students.

It did not take long for me to see who in the class had actual knowledge of either Juvie itself, or some family trauma. I was careful to not push those kids, but I did carefully look at each one, inviting them to stay after and talk to me. Many did.

I put a problem on the board and said to the class, "You, in whatever capacity you are employed, are called to a home. You were told that there has been abuse perpetrated against a child. What do you do?" Now the problem becomes real, as I ask them if they have enough information based on my problem. Would they remove the child, based on my information? I asked for a show of hands. Yes! No! The kids are talking to me, and each other.

We begin to flesh out the information. The child is three months old. Enough? The child is five-years-old. The abuse was the spanking on the rear end, with an open hand. Enough to cite abuse? With a strap. With a paddle. With a belt. An electric cord. The child is ten, and cutting school. The child is twelve, and out of control at school and at home. The child is fifteen, and about to join a gang. What evidence is enough to remove a child from home? How old? What circumstances constitute removal.? I add in drug use, by parent, drug use by child. Now?

In one class, there was one young man sitting in the front. He was very voluble. He talked a lot and added a lot to the discussion. But when I asked for a show of hands as to who was ready to remove or not, and why or why not, he never raised his hand for removal.

No matter what, he would not have removed the child, no matter what the circumstances. Finally, I asked him outright, "Okay then, when is it okay to remove the child?"

The young man cleared his throat and said, "I was raised in a not so good neighborhood. My mother was a single parent and tried to do all she could for me. When I got caught up in the neighborhood, and began to get into trouble, my mom had a red stiletto shoe that she used to hit me with. Now, I got hit pretty often with that red shoe. But, you know what? My friends from my neighborhood are either dead or in jail."

The class and I were silent as the young man continued to speak.

"So I don't have any problem with any of your examples that you said so far."

What this young man said led to a lively discussion of intent, of the differences between discipline with love versus anger and frustration. Because there *are* differences.

But that red shoe example made a mark on me, even to this day

72

You Can Try, but You Can't Save Them All

By now, it should be clear I love my job, the good days, the bad days, the great days, and the awful days. I truly believed, and still do, that saving one family, one child, reverberates through the universe in ways we can't see at the time.

For the most part, the humanity in my courtroom can be reached. Not always to the degree we would want, but even the parents who fail learn something. And we sometimes do not know that, until the next baby comes. And the parents use the new information to regain custody of their child.

So there I was, on just a regular court day, when I got a petition about the Colton family. Twelve children. Six girls named "Kim," six boys named "Jim." Yes, you heard right. We differentiated the children by using middle names, which, thankfully, they had. Mom was a drug user and completely clueless. No dads were around. The kids were raised by nobody.

These kids were in the worst shape I had ever seen. The boys rotated in and out of delinquency, while the girls rotated in and out of maternity wards and with a variety of pimps. The children were all school age. There were no babies, except for the ones the girls kept having. It was a whirlwind of horrible. Chaos times twelve, then fourteen, then fifteen...they really needed a whole court system of their own.

I tried my best with the mother of the dozen plus to at least get her on her feet long enough to feed her own kids. No dice. She wasn't altogether stupid. She knew a time out when she saw it. No kids in her house, they were all in mine. I was begging her to at least take the youngest ones home with her. We'd try it for a month, but then she'd get arrested or the kids weren't eating or going to school, and back into court they would go.

No school, no parenting, no discipline, no nothing. That's what these kids got. I had hoped that placement in good, stable foster homes with normal families would help straighten them out. Give them structure. Give them goals. Nope. You know how in a classroom one kid is proud of his belching? You think all the other kids will make fun of him and he'll stop. You'd be wrong. All the other kids want to learn how to do it. So, from foster home to foster home these kids went, until we weren't sure there were any foster homes left.

When the institutionalized group homes got them, it wasn't for long. The boys, when they got older, were all in delinquency. There, they were in safe hands, sort of. At least we knew where they were. The girls were in a variety of foster and group homes, and further petitions had been filed to remove the babies that kept coming out of them. Incredibly, the mother would come to court to ask for her grandchildren, one at a time. No dice.

As these Kims and Jims aged out of the system, I wondered if I had done any good whatsoever. Just a drop? An iota? I don't think I did though. I think they liked me, for what it was worth. But I was treated like just another adult they got to ignore. It did not matter whether I begged, cajoled, promised, or threatened, nothing would change their history. Or their future. We simply could not offer any possibility of a life they could live. Moment to moment was all they knew.

I had lost. All of them. The girls' babies were adopted out. Some comfort there.

I will say I never saw any of them back in my court again. I guess they just drifted back home one by one. To their mother's house. Where we started years before. Once.

73

We Must Understand Each Other, Regardless of Language

She spoke Japanese. Only Japanese. He spoke Spanish. Only Spanish. Neither spoke each other's language or a common language. No English. And here they were, with their six children, in Juvie.

I honestly do not remember what brought them in. Abuse of some kind? Drugs? I do not think it was domestic violence. Domestic violence allegations tend to stay with you.

I just remember how incredibly bemused I was with this case. Here we were, with two interpreters for the parents, each with his and her own languages, so that they could understand what was happening in court. But how did we get here? How did they meet? How do they make a life day to day without ever understanding the least little thing about each other? Language is key to understanding, I thought. Our hearing-impaired families have sign language to help. Our families where one foreign language is spoken have their six-year-old children interpret for them in the community.

I remember my first husband's grandmother. She never spoke a word of English in her eighty years in this country. She only spoke Yiddish, and never left the neighborhood where that was acceptable. None of her children got past high school. My grandmother, on my dad's side, also spoke Yiddish. And six other languages, all Eastern European, plus a heavily accented English. All of their children went to college.

There was this one case I had with the hearing-impaired young woman who did not, in fact, have sign language to help her. She was developmentally disabled, had not learned sign, and her family never learned either. She had two babies with two men who were long gone. She neglected them, and she really couldn't care for them. Family members were anxious to care for the kids, but they didn't want anything to do with the mother. No one could communicate with her in court. She was ethnically Hispanic and her family members only spoke Spanish. She had never been to school. Diagnosed delayed, hearing impaired, non-English-speaking, it was almost impossible to figure out anything. She didn't understand why the children were gone, she didn't understand where she was, she didn't understand anything. How was I to help?

In her case, I ordered she be immediately enrolled in sign classes. Even if she couldn't read, she could learn to speak through sign. I also ordered that any relative who wanted the children had to also be enrolled. To their credit, one aunt and the grandmother agreed. We could do nothing else until some communication vehicle was found. I set a six-month hearing, and nothing else with a ninety-day interim review to see if any progress was being made. In three months, some very elemental breakthroughs had happened. In six months, they were actually communicating on a very low, but clear level. As if the mother were about three-years-old. This was as good as it got, but the ability to sign to each other made the family decide to allow her to live in a relative's home with the children. I did absolutely nothing legal. Nothing that fit the Juvie requirements. But communication has to be the threshold to maneuver in this world. I thought of Helen Keller, and how smart she turned out to be. This mother did not fit that mold, but living in darkness is not living at all.

About the six-kid family with Momma Japan and Daddy Mexico? They followed all the orders, and regained custody of their children without ever learning each other's language. Since they were educated and could communicate in this world, I didn't order language lessons. Obviously, they negotiated their lives before us, maybe not so well, and would negotiate their lives after us, maybe better.

We take for granted that, for good or evil, we can at least communicate with our environment. Remember this and be grateful, in whatever language that works for you.

74

"Huh?"

I hate to say this, but some of our parents give ignorance a bad name. The difference between not smart and ignorant, is that ignorant is a choice, and some people simply refuse to learn anything. So all I can do is try to separate the ignorance from evil.

The petition in this case was ugly, including past sex abuse, drug use, and healed scars from cigarette burns on the arms of this four-year-old child. She was moved to the home of a close family.

I looked at the petition and right away I saw the problem. In the box for the named father, there were three different names: Jarrod, Troy, James. Now I had mothers who couldn't say at all who the father was, or couldn't say between two, but this lady named three possibilities. One possibility was her current husband, Jarrod, who was long gone but not divorced. He was easy, legally eliminated as he was not cohabitating with the mother at the time of the possible conception. Bye-bye, hubby.

During the lunch hour, I said I would put Mom under oath in the afternoon to clear up this dad business. Paternity determines rights in Juvie.

But over the lunch hour, I heard that Mom grabbed the child in the waiting room and took off. Oh, no. Amber alert? Nope, she was found in less than an hour at the Burger King right around the corner. It seems she was hungry. Had she taken her car, they would have been long gone. If you want to kidnap your child, it's best to actually go somewhere. But back they came, with the sheriff's deputy.

Mom came back into court assuming she was taking her child home. I mean really. She was, however, trying to be cooperative until I put her under oath to determine paternity. Her go-to answer was, "Huh?"

"Who do you believe to be the father of your daughter?" I asked. "Huh?"

Okay, I dropped the word "believed" and substituted "who is."

"Who is the father of your daughter?"

She pointed to the man seated to her right. It was James.

Confused, I asked her, "Then why did you name Troy?"

She looked at me and squinted her face. "Huh?"

We started again. Remember, I have a sexually abused, burned, little four-year-old here, and figuring out the players was taking all my time. I tried not to sigh as I repeated myself.

"Why did you name Troy as the father?"

Well. She indicated that he was the father of her other children, not this one. So, when she got pregnant, she thought she may as well just name him. So he agreed, and signed the birth certificate at the hospital.

"He knows, of course, that he isn't the father," she said.

I looked over at Troy and asked him if he knew he was on the hook for eighteen years.

"Nope," he said.

So we tried again. I asked the mother, "Were you intimate with both of these men at the time of the conception of your child?"

The mother answered, "Huh?"

"Were you sleeping with both of them at the same time?"

The mother answered, "Maybe a couple of times...but there is also Rick."

When the mother named the man, James jumped up.

"Hey! That's my brother!"

The mother laughed. "Oops, I, uh, I was only kidding about him, and don't know why I said his name."

Really? I think we are almost at the end. I named both fathers, Troy and James, as legal fathers, the two in the courtroom, but selected the one we know to be the father, James, and excused the one we know is not the bio father, Troy, the one who signed the birth certificate.

This whole ordeal had taken well over an hour when the mom turned to me.

"So, when can I take my child home?"

I shook my head. "Not today."

The mother then started screaming at the top of her lungs and lunged for the door, ran out, and grabbed her child again. She almost made it to the elevator when she was grabbed by my bailiff. He escorted the mother back into my courtroom, where I ordered that her visits be at the Department of Children and Family Services office only. She was a flight risk.

The mother started screaming at me again. I reiterated the whole reason why we were in the courtroom in the first place.

"Ma'am, you clearly have a complete lack of understanding of the severity of the petition, and refuse to take any responsibility for the abuse to your child. Sexual abuse and burning your child is the problem here."

The mother gave me a blank look. "Huh?"

In all that time in the courtroom, we still hadn't even started to deal with the actual petition. The mother didn't return, and no father ever came to court. The child was adopted by her foster parents.

75

Juvie Folks Always Take Their Work Home

Most people clock out at the end of the day. Once they're off the job, they melt into their own lives. Not me, and not my Juvie colleagues either. We live and breathe our work. Our families are important to us...sometimes to the detriment of our real ones.

Allow me to show you some behind-the-scenes here. We judges spend a lot of time talking about and studying the lifestyles of our court case families. "It takes a village" has since entered the lexicon. We worry about the fact that it is not unusual to have three or more generations of parents and children going through our system. We speculate, psychoanalyze, and discuss. Endlessly.

Any time there were two or more Juvie judges or lawyers together, especially if they were lifers, like me, there it was. Shop talk. It was more than a day job to us. It was a vocation, a calling. We devoted ourselves to improving the lives of these families. Of course, our loved ones sometimes had little patience for our back-and-forth. Spouses and partners would roll their eyes at us. Moratoriums would be agreed to regarding the amount of discussion time that would be tolerated. People of my juvenile ilk would agree to talk about movies, plays, books, current events, travel with our loved ones, but amongst each other, we'd get our fix and talk ad nauseum about our work. Whenever we didn't talk about Juvie, none of us ever lasted very long. We'd go for about ten minutes or so, until some topic reminded one of us about a case we just had, or were wrestling with at the moment, and away we would go again. Locked into our never-ending fascination with the insanity of our jobs and the insanity of those court families.

We talk about new classes, new agencies, new services, new reports, and new studies. We dissect them all. There have been so many instances where our spouses, partners, and non-Juvie friends move away, or talk amongst themselves at a dinner table while we Juvie folks slowly move, circle the wagons, until we are yet again isolated, and talking a mile a minute. The world around us disappears when we talk to each other.

We are a breed apart. As are those families we see in court. We are all in this together. The outcome impacted our self-esteem on both sides of the bench.

We debate judicial styles. How much should we micro-manage these cases? Some of us do all the work, filling out paperwork and forms, so they are up to snuff. Some of us expect our lawyers to provide us with the proper paperwork as it is needed. But paper-filler-outers may not talk to the families, and non-paper-filler-outers may talk extensively directly to them. Some do both, some do neither. What works. We debate compassion versus enabling. And how much personal family information should be shared with Juvie colleagues outside the court case?

I am a non-paper-filler-outer who talks extensively to the families. I talk to the parents, to the children, and then look to the back of the courtroom, to the relatives who came with the parents. I look for nods, I look for a buy-in for the services I will order. I do not believe we should be a competitive system, where each side has to win or lose; in fact, that's what our set of statutes recommends. All sides should be working together to heal the family before us.

Some bench officers believe that the main responsibility lies mostly with the agency who provides the referrals for service. These bench officers are often the hardest on the agency when things go wrong. Some blame only the families, and some are hardest on one or the other parent.

Some courts are boisterous, loud and lively. Lawyers, parents, kids, all get a say. Some are quiet, studious, and respectful in a different, more soothing way. My friends and colleagues run the gamut of personalities and how they believe their courts should run, and how they run them. Some courts are more popular with certain lawyers than others. And, interestingly enough, some lawyers who cannot get along in one court, do extremely well in another.

Each of our courts has a certain ambiance.

It was always amazing to see those families somehow adapt to our environments. Families must trust the court, and most don't, until they are given a reason to believe we believe in and trust them. I've learned that for families to trust us court folks, the dialogue must be free and ongoing. If I said this aloud, which I have, to some of my fellow Juvie friends, some will disagree with me outright. And at yet another dinner party, or gathering, there we'd be, back in the corner again, debating.

76

Being Hated Is Par for the Course

I once had a mother say to me in court, "If I saw you in the desert and you were dying of thirst, I would not spit on you."

Another time, during a hearing, I had another mother say about me: "I see no reason to pay attention to anything said by a person with hair like that. She obviously does not know what she's doing."

Most people think that there is little difference among the players in Juvie. The judge, the attorneys, the social workers are all lumped up into one label: "the system." The system that was designed to take away from them the inalienable right to raise their children as they see fit.

That is especially true for the Judges in Juvie, as we are also the triers of fact, as well as presiding over the trials in terms of what evidence we allow or deny. There are no juries in Juvenile Court, to protect the children's anonymity. There are confidential proceedings not open to the public.

We evaluate evidence and testimony, before trial, and decide what we will allow to be heard. We then hear the trial that we have fashioned, and hear and rule on objections throughout that trial.

Finally, we decide the matter, based on evidence we allow.

No wonder parents cry foul. It seems like everything is stacked against them from the beginning. Parents have a story to tell. It is their story, their lives. To parents, it doesn't matter if their story is irrelevant to the issues. To them, it does not matter if what they have to say is laden with blistering hatred. They need an outlet. They are not mindful, or if they are, don't care that they repeated themselves twenty times to all who would listen, including me.

Whatever story these parents have to tell, it is the job of their attorney to vigorously and zealously represent their clients to the best of ability. A good attorney will be able to take charge of the case, and let the client know what is in his best interests in terms of strategy. A not-so-good attorney believes every word by the client and presents that, or tries to, with no editing at all. Aggressive attorneys do not do their clients any favors by yelling at the judge to impress the client, which is the wrong party to impress. In Juvie, the attorney walks a tightrope between what the client wants and what the client needs. To take control of an angry, hurting parent is no easy task. As the judge, especially where there is no jury, the operative word is "neutral." You cannot help a "newbie" attorney who is pitted against an experienced and wily opponent, regardless of the side they are on.

All I can do is guide the issues. I can ask questions of the witness if I need more information and I think they have it. I observe, I listen, I decide. I explain my decision compassionately, clearly, and cite to the evidence presented. But...I never observe what the parent observes, I never hear what the parent hears. We are on different frequencies.

I've seen grandmothers trying to walk the line between love of a child and love of a grandchild, but the parents saw betrayal in every word. Those times were heartbreaking to watch.

I've seen children afraid to make eye contact with an abusive parent in the courtroom, but the parent saw a bunch of court strangers coaching or bullying the child to act afraid.

I've seen relatives speak out against a parent, so to protect the child, but the parent saw an agenda from the relatives and would ostracize them.

I've seen children called to testify against the parents they love.

While families tend to view "the system" as the enemy, the awful truth of Juvie is that it is mostly family against family.

230

But what unites families is their collective hatred toward me and my judicial peers or anyone from "the system." Usually, I was a much easier target than their family members, or themselves. And when they get their children back, some occasionally thank me for my treatment of them. In those moments, I tell them they did all the work, and deserve all the credit. I only served as a guide, whether they hated me or not. As a judge in Juvie, you will feel a thousand feelings and thoughts each day. But no matter what, at the end of the day, only one counts: Are the children safe?

77

Being Poor
Should Never Be a Cause for Removal

The removal of children from abusive homes is governed by a specific and exhaustive Child Welfare Code. It delineates criteria and sets out the steps necessary to both remove the children safely from their homes, and detain them safely in another home. Then the Department of Children and Family Services (DCFS) have forty-eight court hours to investigate the case and determine whether or not to file a petition in court.

DCFS has several options during the investigation:
1. Return the children and end the investigation.
2. Return the children and provide assistance informally.
3. Detain the children with relatives, or in foster care, and file a petition.

The social worker that responds to a hotline call chooses which option to take. The age and experience of the social worker, the common sense and the sense of compassion, or sense of bull-o-meter, are all factors behind that critical decision. Cynicism sometimes plays a part, as does dewy-eyed optimism.

But the unspoken and unacknowledged elephant in the room is poverty. Lack of money breeds the kind of living conditions and behaviors which lead to abuse. Generations of families incarcerated one by one, or more, criminal activity, skewed values, barriers to education—which includes schools rife with gang activity, and neighborhoods where just stepping out of your front door could be fatal. It is easy to say that education will help break the cycle, but actually making education a safe and rewarding experience is not easy.

And so, sadly, the cycle continues.

Sometimes, we do get wealthy families, but they are very few and far between. We got those families because of horrible, abusive divorces which emotionally harm the children. False allegations of abuse or neglect by one parent against another spill over into dependency from family law. Drug use by famous people which hits the front pages and *People* magazine are in our "confidential" court. Most wealthy families can provide DCFS with a safe, alternate scenario for the children while they deal with the allegations. The less money we have to spend, the more we have for the families who need the most help. Because of this financial reprieve, wealthy families sometimes get a pass a poorer family will not get. Any wealthy family can relocate their children or leave them home with a nanny in the house. Or immediately get into rehab, for example.

But sometimes the wealth gap was glaring, clearly the main factor for a petition, and that was unacceptable!

There was once a very young couple with a very young baby. The couple looked about twelve, but were in their early twenties. The baby was six months old. They had been on the road when they had to pull over. There was a problem with the car. The baby was in a car seat in the back, which wasn't properly engaged with the back seat. While they were taking the baby out of the car, the car seat slipped out and, with the baby still strapped in, fell to the ground. The baby hit his head and was taken from the fallen seat. The parents took the child to the doctor as soon as they were able to procure transportation. The clinic doctor assured the parents that the baby was fine, and told them what to watch for in the next day or so. At some point, however, a social worker got involved, and two days later, a scared, crying young couple presented themselves to my court.

I read the petition, and the supporting documents, and looked at the room. I asked how the baby was, and the answer was "fine." I took a deep breath. When I took a deep breath, all my lawyers knew to take a deep breath as well. And off we went. I yelled at the lawyers for the DCFS.

"If this family had lived in Beverly Hills, this petition would have never been filed! You know this. This family has had two days of hell because some social worker didn't bother to really look at this case with the respect it deserved!"

The young couple, who looked frightened and had their heads hung low, were suddenly looking up at me. I continued.

"These people did everything right. Why are they here!?!"

The DCFS lawyer could not come up with a decent argument. I immediately returned the baby, and by law had to set another date. I assured the young couple that at the next date the petition would be dismissed. They left the courtroom crying, but this time with relief.

There are many people who blame anybody and everybody for their circumstances, and never take responsibility for anything, including appropriately parenting their children. They come in all sizes, shapes, colors, and bank accounts. Then there are those people who do the best they can with inadequate housing, crime-filled neighborhoods, and three jobs. I pledged in heart and mind to know the difference and hope that my fellow Juvie colleagues and DCFS use the same discretion.

78

The Life and Death Cases

If you are a judge who moves money from one rich person to another rich person, or corporation, your days may be filled with drama, as one well-paid attorney after another tries to earn those fees. The outcome will actually affect many people, including company workers and investors in the company stock, leading to a possible ouster of key personnel, and daily headlines.

My job in Juvie does not generate headlines, until another dead baby or child is found, killed by a parent or parent's boy or girlfriend. Then the system kicks into high gear, blame is laid, and the horse-has-left-the-barn investigation begins and the questions from the media come fast and furious:

How many calls were ignored?

How many social workers went out to the home and found nothing?

Did the social worker interview the child with the parents present?

Did the social worker even go inside the house?

The media story churns on, until it gets stale.

But there were cases I heard frequently which never were reported, and got no press. These cases were the worst to the best. By making certain orders, I made the decision that either ended lives or provided a life for others.

Yes, literally life or death decisions.

There was one type of case that we were all heartsick about. The facts varied but led to one conclusion. Something the parent, babysitter, or other person had done to a child, usually a baby or toddler, had left the child on life support. At some point, it became clear that the child was unresponsive, and there was no brain function. The time had come to either withhold sustenance, or withdraw life support, or both. The child would be allowed to die. However, due to religious beliefs, or more prosaic reasons, the parents refused to consent. Of course, if they did, the allegations against them would go from child abuse or endangerment to homicide. So a petition was filed to ask me to make the decision. My heart sank each time I saw one of those petitions.

In those particular cases, we'd hold a trial whereby doctors testified, scientific information was presented, levels of responsiveness were argued. After hearing everything, I'd then make the decision. The parents wept, each and every time. Voices were soft, information was dispassionate, but we were talking about the child here, and we all knew it. A life shortened by the anger, or spite, or negligence of the person supposed to care for you. Those were the most devastating cases to hear. One infant was on life support after it appeared to be a shaken baby incident by a parent. The doctor testified, "This child was in agony. She was fed by a tube and had no possible quality of life or recovery of any kind."

The other side of that coin has to do with the petitions filed to ask me to order lifegiving medical treatment to children or young adults with a life-threatening illness whose parents objected on religious grounds. Most of these kinds of petitions dealt with blood transfusions. Most hospitals now have a protocol in place which can bypass parental consent when necessary, so in my later years, I've seen these cases less and less.

I was the only court to hear those types of life and death cases for several years. I had worked with the religious community attorneys and our own lawyers to come up with a cohesive method of dealing with the life-or-death cases when they came to court. Mostly the parents were not present, just the lawyer. I'd read the petition and ordered the treatment. But some parents did not have a lawyer, so they were appointed one at court, and were therefore present. In those instances, usually, arguments were made, I must say not very forcefully, before I made the orders, and set a new date to make sure the child was out of the woods, or still needed ongoing treatment. I would also check in with the parents, and encourage and support their child's health. On one occasion, the young woman, undergoing treatment for cancer, was found to be cancer free, and came to court to say hello. I was overwhelmed by the graciousness of the parents to let me see this success story, and rejoiced with them.

These questions of life and death never made headlines, but it was probably better that way.

79

The Real Reason Why I Retired

My career in Juvie was magical. The practice did not get me down, and on the bench, I truly loved working with families in need. I was asked to guest edit several publications and books, and I wrote two online courses, which I wrote in longhand, sent back, and the geniuses in San Francisco at the State Bar put online. I taught new judges, chaired several committees, wrote several new forms for use at court, and was asked to lecture throughout the country. My resume was edited, and edited again, as the list of events got longer. I was and I remain the only referee to be named the California Juvenile Court Judge of the year. I had dozens of letters and cards from families and professionals all thanking me for helping them.

It was an honor and a privilege to serve them.

Of course, I had my detractors. I was loud, passionate, animated, active, and, well, shall we say, very East Coast. Families who didn't get what they wanted were always quick to blame the system, which included me. But in my decades of service, I got very few letters of blame or complaints from families about my work. So you can imagine my shock when I was served with a formal complaint alleging "a pattern of unjudicial behavior." I knew I had a powerful enemy in the system, but since no one had ever discussed my demeanor with me before, I felt ambushed. had an easy repartee with my lawyers from the time I had a panel in my court. I also got along with the new system of agency lawyers, but I did not call them by their first names or have lunch with them outside court.

The rumor mill spread the word about me, and I started hearing that there was a concerted effort to collect any behavior of mine which could be construed as inappropriate. This movement, for the first time in my decades of working the bench, slowed me down, made me second guess myself. I was uncharacteristically on edge, which was probably the goal. A list was generated by one disgruntled ex-attorney, and that constituted the complaint. I had had friends who went through similar situations, but this felt different. It felt personal. And it was. She and I clashed regularly regarding my concern about her ability to protect children. I had heard that none of my current attorneys would testify against me, which was heartening. However, that one former attorney in my court, couldn't wait to slander me.

Two things happened quickly. As a subordinate bench officer, I had no right to a hearing, a lawyer, or any rights other than to answer the complaint in writing, item by item. Outraged and embarrassed, I denied almost all the allegations. One or two were accurate, but out of context. Secondly, and unusually, a local legal newspaper printed I was in this position, before any findings were made. No reputable newspaper ever printed allegations, and in this case, no other newspaper ever did. I heard my own rumors that the disgruntled lawyer knew the writer, but had no idea if that were true. Normally, I would be yesterday's news quickly, but because of social media, that small article remained for all to see, just by looking up my name.

After I submitted my defense, the judgment came: I was suspended for a month, and had to take one class on judicial demeanor. I had a response to this answer: I quit.

I did not resign.

I quit.

But my presiding judge talked me out of it.

Nearly three decades of a spotless national reputation, and now this.

So, I did my time, took my punishment, and returned to my court. By this time, I was really angry. I did not do what they found I did.

The context was ignored, the emotion was ignored, the actual facts were ignored. What they finally found was nothing like what was in the newspaper, but there was no follow-up by the paper. I sat on the bench watching every word I said. What I hoped was powerful and different about me on the bench was my informality, and engagement with the families. I talked to them, giving my opinion, giving encouragement, giving verbal spankings, right from the first day. I never held back. If I could ease a mind, I did it. If I was disgusted with the behavior, I said it. I told them clearly, concisely, and immediately what I wanted to have happen. And I used humor as much as I could, even in dire circumstances, to try to reach the humanity in the families. If relatives were there, I talked to them about support, and protecting the children.

But that was the old me. After the reprimand, I became a shell of my former self. I was a robot on the bench. I was exactly the kind of judge who should never be in Juvie. A cold, removed, literal interpreter of the law. Dry, closed, in pain every day. About six months later, I decided to retire. My heart simply wasn't in it anymore. I told my bosses and gave a date a few months later in order to take advantage of financial considerations. My friend Jacque asked me if I wanted to a goodbye party. I said I would like a small goodbye from my friends at court, but if she didn't get enough people to come, we could just have a lunch with my close friends. I didn't bring it up again as I was a little scared to ask.

While I was dying inside, the backlash was immediate and ferocious. I was too miserable to do anything but go, like a sick cat, into a corner and lick my wounds. Others, however, were furious on my behalf. The wave of support was like a tsunami.

My colleagues on the bench, throughout California, lawyers inside the courthouse, social workers, clerks, and lawyers placed in my court were livid and vocal. Not a day went by without some message of strength and positivity. I also got other words of encouragement.

"Sherri, snap out of it! You aren't the first judge who has been disciplined, and you won't be the last."

"Some people are saying you should treat it like a badge of honor because you did it your way."

"You took what they gave out, and now it's time to be yourself again."

In the beginning, nothing helped. But over time, slowly, I eased back into Sherri.

When my friend Jacque told me she rented a room in a restaurant, I breathed a sigh of relief. About fifty people had responded to the invitation.

I was at least somewhat still liked and respected.

But more than fifty people came. In fact, there were 130 people from San Diego, Orange County, Los Angeles, from court, and dozens of community agencies I had worked with over the years. I was overwhelmed. I remember almost nothing about the evening, other than profound gratitude. That evening was beautiful but also a blur. I was told my speech was powerful and affirming. I don't remember what I said. I received many awards and plaques. I don't remember what they said, but I remember I cried a lot.

The next day, Friday, was my last day on the bench. I did my calendar, and my whole court gave another private party. We all cried.

The Indian community also asked to honor me, with a luncheon, a drumming, and a blanket wrap. It was an amazingly moving ceremony. The food was all handmade. The drum was huge, surrounded by several men, all drumming and chanting at the same time. It beats with your heart, and you become a part of the whole. Then, after speeches and gifts, I was wrapped in a beautiful Pendleton blanket. I was then led from the room, wrapped and protected by the tribe.

I cried a lot. The outpouring of love and support meant so much to me but underneath it all, even underneath the gratitude, I couldn't shake off the shame that led to my early retirement.

My children didn't even know the real reason why I retired.

Months after I retired, I was asked to present at a juvenile symposium at Whittier Law School. I was to give an hour-long presentation on the ins and outs of a juvenile practice. I was third on the agenda, and could see by the end of the second speech, that interest in the room was waning. I decided then and there to abandon my notes, and just talked. I talked from the heart and I didn't hold back. I talked about the realities of the job, about the families, about dedication and frustration. Up there, on that podium, I felt like my old self again.

At the lunch break, the organizer of the symposium came up to me.

"You know, when you were suggested as an expert, I looked you up and I saw the newspaper article. I have to admit, I had doubts. But I was persuaded to stay with you and I cannot tell you how glad I am I did."

My blood stopped. I felt many emotions in that split second with the symposium organizer. White-hot embarrassment and red-hot rage. All those many years of good work soiled by someone with a personal vendetta who filed a complaint? Was this really something that was going to follow me for the rest of my life? Was that going to be what I was known for!?! I had so much to say in that moment to the symposium organizer. More than I could verbally say. But instead, I smiled.

"Well. Thanks for having me today." And with that, I walked away.

It's been years since I retired and that article came out. I still occasionally sit on assignment as needed at court. That complaint, along with the article, is like a distant memory to everyone but me.

I still live with the shame of it despite all the warm love I have received from the court, the families, the people. I wish I could say the love has swallowed up the shame, but it hasn't.

It just hasn't.

80

Those 3 a.m. Thoughts

Ever wonder what goes on inside the mind of a judge? It's not unusual to be up at 3 a.m., going over in my brain the life-changing decisions I made earlier in the day. My day job consists of a never-ending onslaught of the issues that keep coming in the most traumatic ways. First comes the case facts, then the judicial questions:

How addicted was this addict, with what substance, for how long?

How hard and why was this child hit? With what? How often?

This family are immigrants, with language issues, and different ways of living, they have a different culture than ours. They don't see what they're doing as "abuse."

Is this domestic violence or mutual war?

If the abuser is out of the home, in jail, does it make a difference?

On the issues of molest, we factor in age, proximity of relationship, and how often the abuse occurred into our decisions.

No stone is left unturned in Juvie. We have seen it all and then some. If it would never occur to you, we have seen that too.

Behind every decision that you think is a no-brainer, let me throw in a bit of an idea you didn't think about. We do not have children clamoring for our help. Praying for our intervention. We have abused, traumatized children and youth who are now pulled from family, friends, school, activities, because, yes, in the midst of the trauma, life goes on in some way. They have normalized their chaos.

With every decision to remove or not remove, we can be universally hated by all. And we do the best we can, from our hearts, if we care enough to be here. It must be tougher, or maybe not, for those who don't want to be here.

In the middle of the night, my mind has raced with the second-guessing.

Did I do the right thing?

Did I remove too quickly?

Could something have been done to keep the kids home?

Did I jump from my own response to a parent who reacts and spews vitriol, or angry denial?

Am I expecting remorse and willingness to get help every time?

Did the fact that the parent was sobbing and promising an immediate change alter my decision to remove and allow the children to stay or go home too soon?

And the answer is yes. I am wrong. Both ways. I have been wrong enough times that it keeps me up at 3 a.m. But I have also been right. More times than not right. I do not know in those 3 a.m. spirals, but I later learn the vitriolic parent is immediately and successfully engaged in rehabilitation, or that the sobbing mom in the courtroom let the abuser back into the home that very night. And the fourteen-year-old who promised to stay on track actually is now on the run, whereabouts unknown.

I do the best with what I know is in front of me. I always operate with the best intentions, but I am human. They are human. Case closed.

I have been fortunate enough to have new judges in my courts who make the legal rounds before they find assignments. I talk to them in chambers and ask about their possible interest in Juvie. Most are not interested—to them, I say to find some work with kids for their souls.

To those interested in Juvie, I share the heartache and full heart of this incredible career. Some come, some don't; some stay, some don't. Either way, our kids keep coming. And we keep working and hoping for the best.

81

For Thirty Years

For thirty years, I have worked in child welfare. I have represented parents, kids, teens, grandparents, and foster parents. I have run the gamut of perpetrators, victims, liars, deniers, and family members involved, as well as those not involved. This is high drama on steroids. Every day, case after case after...

I sympathized, tried to show my caring, and conveyed my complete wish for their success. I was attempting to get that buy-in so necessary for change. I could separate the acts from the person, at least most of the time, and let them see that I was rooting for a reunion. I wanted the kids to know that I was hoping their parents would do what they needed to do. So, along with reunification and/or permanency, I believed in a third prong: one that was focused on the children and youth getting an education and having someone supportive of them.

As a lawyer, a bench officer, and a judge, I did everything I could do. I did my best every day. I read the books, took the classes, and ingrained in my full brain the following mantras:

"Every child needs one important person who believes in him, her, or them."

"Relapse is part of recovery."

"Children will pine for home, regardless of what home is like."

I studied and learned about the changes that occur in children's brains when they witness domestic violence. Children are even affected by domestic violence in the womb. I heard "this system works" or "that system works," we changed modalities each year as new studies appeared.

But what do we know? We know that children in the system feel that no one in the world cares about them, that the loss of family, parents, siblings, aunts, uncles, cousins, and friends at school is crippling. Trying to ensure caring in a courtroom setting, a foster home, or a group home is simply not enough. We have had some success and breakthroughs in getting kids to loving and stable homes, saving them from living out another generational cycle. We have had youth who found the inner strength they needed to walk their own path, love their parents, forgive, and move on. They took advantage of what was offered and forged a new life, identifying with their strength and fortitude.

It's safe to say that I've seen it all in the thirty years of overseeing court proceedings, making placement decisions, conducting review hearings to assess the progress of cases, ensuring timely resolutions, and coordinating with other agencies, all in the best interests of the child. It has been an honor to be in a position to right some wrongs in these children's lives. While it was never easy to hear what children of abuse, neglect, and endangerment go through, my job (our job as a system) is nothing in comparison to what kids in foster care have endured and will carry with them lifelong. That realization has never escaped me. I saw the children's faces behind their case files, and their stories will forever live with me.

Index

Dependency At a Glance

Detention

Department of Children and Family Services (DCFS) has had a report of abuse, molest, or neglect. They have investigated and found the reports true. They have determined that a voluntary contract for services with the family will not alleviate the danger to the children. They file a petition in Juvenile Court. This is the family's first appearance in court. The children are in foster care, or with appropriate relatives. The Court must decide whether or not to return the children, with services to the family, or keep the children out of the home. Reunification services are ordered.

Jurisdiction

This is the hearing at which parents can plead to the allegations (either straight up or amended) or set a trial to have the Department prove its case. The Court makes its findings by a preponderance of the evidence.

Disposition

At this hearing, legal and physical custody is determined. The standard is clear and convincing evidence to remove the children from the custody of their parents. If the children are returned, the Court can exit out of the case, or provide maintenance services to help the family. If the children are not returned, the Court may, or may not, provide reunification services to assist in regaining custody. Issues of relative placement are determined here, and issues of non-offending parents, and parentage/status issues are also determined.

Six-Month Review

This is the first mandatory review to determine how the family is doing. If the children are over the age of three, services will most likely continue for six months, if the parents do not regain custody. If the parents do regain custody, the Court will provide maintenance services for six months. If any one of the children is under the age of three, the Court can choose to stop reunification services and move on to a permanent plan.

Twelve-Month Review

This is the second mandatory review. The Court can return children; not return children, and find a final six months of services would be likely to return the children; or cut to a permanent plan.

Eighteen-Month Review

The final reunification hearing. Return, or set an implementation hearing to establish a permanent plan of long-term foster care, planned permanent living arrangement, legal guardianship, or adoption.

Implementation Hearing

This hearing determines the final plan for the child. Adoption is the first choice for permanency, legal guardianship is second, planned permanent living arrangement is third, long-term foster care is the least preferred plan.

Post-Permanency Hearings

We keep jurisdiction over some of our children until they emancipate. Age eighteen is a guideline, but not necessarily fixed. We can keep children until they turn twenty-one, if necessary.

Other Issues

Parentage, Indian Status, Education, Relative Issues, Change of Order (388) hearings.

Appendix

Over the decades on the bench, I have received hundreds and hundreds of examples of what I like to call "physical evidence that we make a difference in the lives of children." Throughout the years, my heart has been deeply touched by each drawing, note, and letter from children in Juvie. Because it's about love after all, I would like to end this book with the personal expressions from some of the children who have been in my courtroom.

Judge can you bring us togther agirn becaus we me's my DaD and mom wech my mom is whith us but my Dad isint whith us. To. Judge
  from.

✶✶✶✶✩

Dear, Judge
cAn we please
go home I mean
we been in
foster homes
since 6 and half
months I
mean every body
misses us
in are family
you know your
the best Judge
that any kid
ever had.
Always

Dear Judge,

I wanna thank you for all you've done for me and my sisters and brother and mom I am so happy that learned more how to take care of us. When she got us back I was the proudest big sister ever ☺ I thank you for all that you've done for her too. I'm doing good in school getting good grades. Anyway THANKS Judge

Yours Truly,

Dear Judge,
I ♡ you ☺!
For everything
you've did for
my mom :)

FROM:

You're Honor,

My Mother can be a handful at times, but she only does it because she loves us so very much. We love her as much as she loves us, she's our Mom no matter what you do or say you can't change it. She's still our Mom. My mom may take things a little harder than others, but that's how you know she does care about us. She may not think things over before said... But knowing my mom she will say or do anything to get us back. She raised us very well and made us to who we are today; Well behaved, smart, Respectful, and courteous to all others.

I want to be with my mom again. I may not show it but I appreciate everything my mom has, and will do for me... ███ if it's a simple "Goodnight". There is no person who can take the place as my Mom. She really is the missing piece of my heart. She has been taken out of part of my life, but soon my brothers too? I would not want them taken from me too. People may think its "Best" for them to be adopted, but you're ripping our family... Slowly and Painfully. You have asked us if we would want to be with our mom. Yes, we do. She raised us from scratch. And we came out wonderful children... Have we not? And it's all because of our Wonderful Mother. She's understands us, as do we towards her. My mom has made mistakes. But haven't we all? She's only human... A human who wants her family back. My Mom also has to understand she has to try to work with the system to get us back. Not everything will land in your lap if you just ask. Sometimes you have to work hard to get the things you truly love.

I used to think my Mom, two Brothers, and sister was my only Family. But I realized Family does not necessarily mean blood related. Family is someone who does care for you no matter what and loves you unconditionally... And apparently I have a bigger family then I ever thought I did. Ones I know care for me just as much as my mom does. And I'm great full for them. They take care of me as if I was there own. I used to think my mom was the only one who I truly could love and count on. But I have ████████████████████████████████████ and many more People. And I never knew I could have had this many people who could ever love me for me besides for my mom. They are my home away from home ... and I believe a home is somewhere someone is always thinking of you. I know all these people think about me...But my Mom is always thinking about me she is my Home... That's where I know we belong.

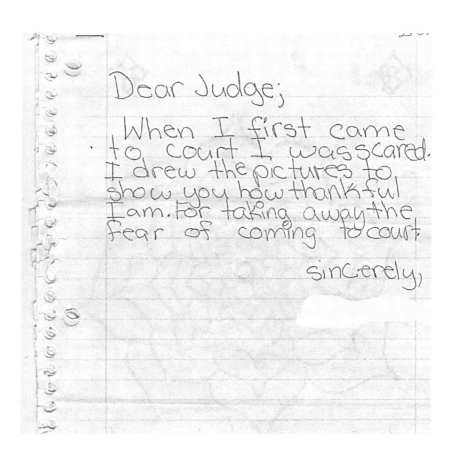

Dear Judge;

When I first came to court I was scared. I drew the pictures to show you how thankful I am. For taking away the fear of coming to court.

sincerely,

Acknowledgements

To my Developmental Editor, Georgette Todd, also the author of *Foster Girl, a Memoir*. Simple. No Georgette, no book.

And to Laura Duffy for her wonderful book cover.

And to Brooks Becker for copyediting.

To Los Angeles Juvenile Court, the largest in the world, who took a chance and gave me a job. Thanks Mike, Marilyn, and my wonderful colleagues. Special hugs to Jacque, Zeke, and Tony. No job, no book.

To Osher Lifelong Learning Institute (OLLI), senior learning classes, and my wonderful colleagues in the memoir class. No class, no book.

To my mother, Ruth, who always had Charles Chips, and room for one more at the table.

To my father, Lee, who signed me up for the book-of-the-month club when I was born. And thought I was truly terrific. No matter what.

To Craig, my first reader and best cheerleader, love of my life, you are on every page.

To the thousands of families who enriched my life by sharing their stories with me, whether they wanted to or not.

And, finally, to any reader I have out there. Please remember we are all a family, and do what you can. Bless you all.

Here Are Ways
You Can Help Kids in Foster Care

1. Get involved with your entire family. Stay in touch with everyone. Butt in where necessary. If trouble is brewing, make your presence known, but don't wait until things blow up. Talk things out with the parents. Be there for the children.

2. Volunteer with a community organization that supports foster students, as they often face isolation and loneliness as significant challenges. These young individuals require compassionate individuals to step forward as friends and advocates, demonstrating that they are valuable and that their futures are worth fighting for. If you happen to reside in the Los Angeles area, spanning from Lancaster to Long Beach, California, I supervise an educational project called "Education Rights Holders," offering a fantastic opportunity to become an educational advocate for children who lack one. Training is always provided, and backup assistance is available. To begin your journey, please contact my dear friend, Paul Freese, at pfeese27@outlook.com. Paul is a retired public interest lawyer and child welfare advocate who can provide you with more information on how to become an Education Rights Holder for foster students.

3. Speaking of Paul...you can start a "Simply Friends" group. Simply Friends is a program he helps lead inspired by Mr. Rogers, who asked the question, "Won't you be my neighbor?" Simply Friends organizes individuals with a heart for foster kids to offer friendship through social visits in their

group home settings and help them appreciate that they have neighbors who care. Food and friendship are the currency that build trust and more enduring relationships. Many Simply Friends participants take the next step to become court appointed Education Rights Holders for foster students. Many former foster youth join Simply Friends social visits and they bring food, games, activities and simply have fun together. As one former foster youth said, "Just visit like you would visit your best friends and hang out with us!" To get involved, reach out to Paul or visit the Simply Friends website: www.SimplyFriends.org

4. If you are actively involved in a faith-based community, organize and reach out to families in need. The better the response, the less chance for children to be in the system! See if your church can join Care Portal to add to its network of providing help to families. Care Portal uses technology that drives action for local children and families in crisis. Here is their website to learn more: www.CarePortal.org

5. You can enroll as a Court Appointed Special Advocate (CASA), a national organization that provides court advocacy for foster kids. This program only requires ten hours of volunteer time a month. To get started, you can go to their website: www.NationalCASA.org

6. You can also consider adopting an older child, a child with disabilities, or a sibling set. These kids are often the most neglected in foster care, and they deserve a better life, too.

7. If you work in child welfare or are a CASA, please visit Connect Our Kids at www.ConnectOurKids.org. They develop and provide free and low-cost advanced family search and engagement software that can help you quickly discover and

organize a child's immediate and extended family, friends, and network. To learn more about this innovative way to identify and locate a child's family, you can email them at Hello@ConnectOurKids.org.

8. If you see something, say something to the family, to the school, and, if necessary, to law enforcement. Protect our kids.

9. If direct advocacy isn't your thing, you can always donate to an organization that helps foster kids. Any organization I mentioned in this list is a good start.

10. If you cannot donate your time, talent, or treasure, I encourage you to increase your knowledge and spread the word. Please let people know what foster kids go through. You can recommend books like this one and encourage them to get involved in their own families and communities. It may take a village, but it starts with you. Thank you.

Made in the USA
Las Vegas, NV
07 November 2024

11254738R00163